HERITAGE OF BRITAIN

Above The Lord Mayor's Coach and Pikemen of the Honourable
Artillery Company at the Law Courts, part of the Lord Mayor's Show
in London.

Overleaf The Lion Bridge and the Castle at Alnwick, Northumberland.

Endpapers Buckingham Palace, London.

HERITAGE OF BRITAIN

A. L. Rowse

TREASURE
PRESS

CONTENTS

1 PREHISTORY AND EARLY INFLUENCES

page 7

2 CAPITALS AND REGIONAL CENTRES

page 35

3 CITY AND COUNTRY LANDMARKS

page 65

First published in Great Britain by Artus Books Ltd
and distributed by Marks & Spencer Ltd

This edition published by Treasure Press
59 Grosvenor Street
London W1

© 1977 A. L. Rowse

Reprinted 1984

ISBN 0 907407 58 7

Printed in Hong Kong

4 DEFENCES AND DWELLINGS

5 SEATS OF PRAYER AND LEARNING

6 TECHNOLOGY AND THE ARTS

ACKNOWLEDGMENTS

INDEX

1 PREHISTORY AND EARLY INFLUENCES

THE HISTORY OF BRITAIN has been one of the most interesting and successful stories in the world; and the island has the richest inheritance of any island, historically and visually. One of the joys of inhabiting an old country is that it is feet deep in the sediment of centuries, of memories and associations, monuments, relics, reminders. Wherever one turns, if one has an eye to see and a mind to explore, there are the memorials of former peoples – a barrow or tumulus on the skyline, a bend in the road revealing the curve of a prehistoric round camp; standing stones, monoliths, hut-circles, where these folk lived and worshipped. There are their artefacts and utensils – which have their own interesting evolutions – their pottery and metal work, their bronze and silver and jewellery to appreciate and enjoy, thousands of years after these things were made. Archaeology is a living and popular pursuit today; but history has this advantage over it, that archaeology can scarcely enter the minds and thoughts of our ancestors. History can.

Prehistory is, of course, continuous with history; underneath the skin of the present one can often see the prehistoric surviving. One can glimpse it, with any imagination, in people. No animal has such a range of difference and diversity, of capabilities and inequalities, as man.

The historic legacy is, however, much richer and more varied than the prehistoric. One can hardly deny the term architecture to such astounding achievements of barbaric peoples as Stonehenge and Avebury – we see only the ruins of them today; but historic architecture offers us much greater variety. Again, wherever we are in an old country we are surrounded by memorials that speak to us – Roman villas, temples, forts, monuments; Anglo-Saxon or medieval churches, cathedrals, monasteries; castles, fortresses, palaces, country houses of all periods; universities and colleges bequeathed by the Middle Ages or later; in the churches, the tombs of the people who left us these things; their portraits, pictures, possessions, archives; their letters, their literature; their language (or languages), with their layers of sediment, too, the evidences of their changes of inflexion and usage, fossils of speech. With these we are entering the inner world of the mind, the legacies of the spirit, with which we are not primarily concerned here.

All this adds a whole dimension to our mental experience and enjoyment of life. But we can do nothing like justice to it all; we can only select and suggest, hoping to be at the least representative. To select the best, and most significant, of men's achievements seems the fairest course and offers most promise. Helpfully for our purpose, societies are remembered on the whole for the finest of their products, their works of genius, their most outstanding spirits, not for the commonplaces of every day. Those we have always with us, and they are not memorable: they simply recur.

We shall then be concerned with what stands out, with what is exceptional, that which has often survived *because* it is exceptional and has been prized through the ages.

THE VERY INSULARITY of the island has been the dominant factor through all the later stages of men's story in Britain, right up to yesterday: most significantly, in 1940. The easily navigable, indeed the inviting, waters around the islands have proved no impassable bar to invaders, but they have imposed some impediment (again until recently), some time-lag which has sifted invaders, given the geographical conditions a chance to work upon them and enabled incoming peoples to meet their challenge with deferred responses and work out appropriate solutions. Wave after wave of migrants have come in, each making its own contribution to the creative whole, leaving its silt of cultural products, its evidences and relics to the general legacy. Insularity modified the cultures and traditions of the Continent, so that the island and its inhabitants developed their own character and distinctive traits – a process going on all through history.

We are not concerned with the shell-heaps of neolithic peoples, primitive hunters before men learned to cultivate the soil and build, or with the remains of their caverns and holes –

Previous pages Prehistoric Stonehenge, Salisbury Plain, on midsummer morning.

The White Horse, at Westbury, Wiltshire.

such as the caverns at Torquay, which upset the obstinate objection to the facts of evolution, places like Wookey Hole in the Mendips, or the caves of Derbyshire. It happens that in Stonehenge and Avebury the island possesses the finest prehistoric monuments in Europe.

Stonehenge is the more familiar and sensational, often described and painted, as in Turner's and Constable's watercolours. The subtlety and complexity of this extraordinary monument preclude detailed description here. It was being built and reshaped during three distinct periods over several hundred years, longer than was the case with most medieval cathedrals, though during its successive transformations the main axis always remained aligned to midsummer sunrise. The last stage in its shaping seems to have been about 1900 to

The stone circle at Avebury, Wiltshire, is the largest in Britain, now encroached upon by the village. The circle encloses an area of 28 acres; it was probably constructed in the Late Neolithic period.

1500 BC, when 'a pitch of architectural refinement was achieved unparalleled in the prehistoric West'. These huge stones have almost imperceptible swelling like Greek columns, the architrave curves inward to make a circle, the laterals are morticed and tenoned to fit the uprights and shaped to the perspective from the ground. An inner circle was formed of bluestones brought all the way – 200 miles – from Wales. All around are the cemeteries of these people, some three hundred barrows; a long avenue of stones went down to a stream. All this is not only a standing witness to what primitive manpower could shift – that is obvious enough – but a marvel of sophisticated planning and design.

Archaeologists find Avebury, not far away, even more impressive. 'In its final form this temple comprised two pairs of concentric circles of huge stones weighing many tons apiece, standing within a single stone circle, the largest of its kind in Europe, which was itself enclosed by a vast ring ditch-embanked. Southward an avenue of pairs of stones follows a slightly zig-zag course down to the River Kennet, and thence to Overton Hill, where it terminates in another sacred enclosure.' Impressive as it is in its geometry, what we see today is again only a fragment of what once was. Originally there were many more stones; numbers have been broken up for various uses, some were deliberately buried by medieval folk in holes dug for them because of the hoodoo upon them. (A woolman of the time of Edward III was in one of the pits when an enormous stone toppled in upon him.)

A mile from Avebury, in this chalk upland country of the Wessex culture, is unique Silbury Hill. 'One hundred and thirty feet high, with a base covering more than five acres, it is the largest artificial mound in Western Europe.' What adds to the uniqueness of this pyramid is its mystery archaeologically: though it has several times been scratched, rather than probed in depth, nothing has ever been found to explain it. Here is what the historian finds frustrating in archaeology. Nevertheless, the whole of these uplands – so beloved of Richard Jefferies, the life of their later folk described with intimate understanding in his books – was evidently the scene of a brilliant primitive culture in these islands. The mingling of peoples was at its best here: the small dark Mediterranean people from the west with Nordic stock thus early from across the North Sea – comparable to the two elements which fused to make the creative miracle of ancient Greece.

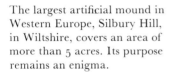

The largest artificial mound in Western Europe, Silbury Hill, in Wiltshire, covers an area of more than 5 acres. Its purpose remains an enigma.

Left The baths at Bath were built over warm natural springs by the Romans, who realized the value of the salts in the water and made the town into the first spa in Britain.

Above Bath was originally named Aquae Sulis after Sul, the native deity, a sort of early British counterpart to the Roman Minerva. This head of Minerva, goddess of handicrafts and arts, is in the Roman Baths Museum at Bath.

map, in river- and hill-names, and embedded in the names of cities, towns, villages, hamlets, farms. Incoming settlers often took over previous names – all part of the rich heritage of which most people are unaware.

Some places carry a great deal of history within them: Lincoln, for instance, so famous to Americans. It comes from Lindum colonia, i.e. the Roman colony at the round-camp, *dum* or *din*, by the pool, *lyn*. The prehistoric settlement occupied the top of the hill, where now stands one of the noblest of medieval cathedrals; part of the Roman gateway into the old town on the east still stands, and an arch through which (light) traffic of near two thousand years after can pass. The name of London is Celtic, with the same elements, the settlement by the pool; so too with such cities as Dover, York and Leeds. Manchester, Winchester, Worcester, Gloucester, Rochester, Exeter betray their history, Celtic – Roman – Anglo-Saxon, from the elements obvious in their names (chester is the English rendering of Roman *castrum*, i.e. camp). The word Glastonbury conveys its own dual origins within it: the Anglo-Saxon camp (*bury*) by the farm (*ton*); *Glas* is the Celtic word for green, which appears again in Glasgow.

Many geographical features retain their old Celtic names – the Pennines, for instance, are cousins of the Appenines; Cumberland (Cumbria) has its affiliation with the Cymric Celts. River names are frequently Celtic: Esk, Exe and Axe, Lea and Dee, Avon, Colne (cf. Colchester) and Cam; it is thought that some river-names are even pre-Celtic, for example, Ouse and Thames–Tamar–Teme.

The names themselves reflect the phenomenon of overlying – the successive layers of sediment left by history upon the land. The amphitheatre at Dorchester overlies a prehistoric henge, or round-camp. William the Norman Conqueror's Tower of London incorporates a bastion of the Roman wall; under the pavements of the City are Roman baths, a Mithraic temple. The recent excavations at York Minster revealed a column of a Roman temple under the crypt. On the headland of Tintagel, which protects a rare landing-beach on that exposed coast, are the ruins of a Norman castle; within that are the cells of a Celtic monastery; around that the embankment of a prehistoric camp. No wonder Celtic memories gathered around that unforgettable spot.

OF ROMAN MEMORIALS that are a living legacy to Britain the most frequently encountered are the roads, the most spectacular the Wall along the Borders, and the most expressive of Roman civilization, Bath. To these we may add among other things, it seems, the pheasant, the cherry and the edible snail. Besides this the Romans, who were here for four hundred years, must have contributed some sperm to the population. Not many of them were Romans proper; the large numbers of troops employed during that period were drawn from all over the empire, from as far afield as Hungary (Dacia) or Spain, but increasingly of Saxon mercenaries:

> *When Severn down to Buildwas ran*
> *Coloured with the death of man,*
> *Couched upon her brother's grave*
> *The Saxon got me on the slave.*

These Germanic people came to see the capabilities of the island before the end. Some of the cities the Romans founded declined or were damaged before the end of the empire: St Albans (Verulamium), Silchester, Caistor, Wroxeter (Viroconium), for example.

> *'Twould blow like this through holt and hanger*
> *When Uricon the city stood ...*
>
> *The gale, it plies the saplings double,*
> *It blows so hard, 'twill soon be gone:*
> *Today the Roman and his trouble*
> *Are ashes under Uricon.*

The prehistoric peoples used the ridgeways along the spines of land up above swamps and thick woodland – like that going down along the spine of Cornwall (A30), or that along the Mendips (where the Romans mined lead) west of Frome (A361). Or there is the admirable turfy track along the Berkshire Downs above Uffington, with the prehistoric horse, carved in the flanks of the chalk hillside, which has given its name to the Vale of the White Horse – and has been kept scoured by unnumbered generations of local folk with traditional rites (described by Tom Hughes of *Tom Brown's Schooldays*).

The Roman roads marched identifiably straight uphill and down dale – though how many people driving about the country recognize them for what they are? Many are overlaid by modern roads – some of the most important, like Watling Street (so called by the Saxons) from Dover to London and thence right across the country, cutting it in half, to Holyhead, the Roman outpost looking across to the provokingly unconquered island of Ireland. Again one recognizes the straight course along the Great North Road towards Corbridge (Corstopitum) and the Wall; or the roads radiating out from Colchester (Camulodunum). I always think of it, after the twists and turns of West Country roads, striking north-east from Exeter along the Fosse Way; at one low-lying spot, where Saxons and medievals neglected to keep the road in repair, the modern track leaves it to make two sides of a triangle before coming back into it again; the Roman is demoted as a green lane. Many more such roads lie unrevealed under the fields, though indications of their whereabouts can be found in the mile-stones of which not a few remain.

The network covered the country like a spider's web, with London at the centre. These roads, and the Thames artery, ultimately established London as the country's centre of trade. The roads connected up the provincial capitals as well as served the frontiers, from legionary bases like York, Chester and Caerleon. Fosse Way marched from Exeter (Isca) to Bath, across the Cotswolds to Cirencester, thence to Lincoln. The Cotswolds were a highly Romanized area – Cirencester one of the largest provincial capitals, practically all of it buried under the medieval town. The region has several large villas – self-supporting estates on their own – of which Chedworth is best known and completely exposed. All round in this

Above left The Roman lighthouse within the walls of Dover Castle, Kent, is called the Pharos, after the famous lighthouse at Alexandria, in Egypt.

Above right Pevensey, in Sussex, the landing-place of William the Conqueror when he invaded Britain in 1066. Although the outer wall is Roman, the ruins are principally of the Norman period and later.

Portchester Castle in Hampshire is a fine example of the mixture of Roman and Norman architecture.

area are their mementoes: fragments of temples and shrines, altars with their inscriptions commemorating the named but unknown dead. However, these remind us that they once were alive here.

Waterways have remained continuously important all through the history of the Lowland Zone of the island, i.e. mainly England. No part of the south-eastern half of Britain is far from communication by water; this has made England a more integrated and united area than the Highland Zone of west and north, and helped it to achieve ascendancy over the rest. Far less familiar than rivers and roads are the remarkable canals the constructive Romans made all round the Wash, turning it into a rich granary. The decline of the empire and the incursion of the barbarians meant the breakdown of these works of civilization, so that the whole area lapsed into the subsequent quagmire of Hereward the Wake, a few islets of monastic cultivation, the misery of unhealthy fenland life, and romantic folklore.

The barbarous Teutonic world posed an increasing threat to Roman civilization and necessitated the fortification of the coast from the Wash to the Isle of Wight (as again in 1940): 'the Saxon Shore'. Remarkable evidences that survive are the great walled fortresses of Richborough, the walls still fairly complete, Pevensey and Portchester. A more affecting memorial is the lighthouse at Dover that lighted ships into the harbour those millennia ago – continuity indeed.

All over the country there are evidences of the Roman occupation of which few people are aware. It used to be thought that the Romans hardly penetrated into remote Cornwall, but recently two characteristic rectangular forts have come to light. Nanstallon near Bodmin was one of a chain of signalling stations that watched the Bristol Channel; Carvossa (i.e. originally a Celtic *caer*, or camp, with ramparts) guarded a creek on the Fal, probably in connection with the tin-trade. The Roman foundations of London Wall were revealed by German bombing in our time. Most fascinating is a trip to Leicester's Jewry Wall, the well preserved remains of the city's Roman Baths, with the nearby Saxon church of St Nicholas largely built out of the stones. At St Albans Cathedral one sees the Roman tiles from Verulamium built into the tower.

Most remarkable of all is Hadrian's Wall. 'Even today, when these vast works remain only in shattered fragments, they are a monument of Roman purposiveness than which none more impressive exists in any country: a fitting memorial to an emperor distinguished above others for his ambition as an architect and his remorseless demands on the labour of his troops.' (London had a colossal bronze statue of him.) The wall extended over 70 miles, from Wallsend on the Tyne to Bowness on the Solway; much of it remained, to astonish an Elizabethan historian like Camden, right up to the eighteenth century, when whole sections were demolished for road-making.

It still makes its staggering impression as one looks out from its top over the wild 'debatable land', previously inhabited by wilder tribesmen. Away farther to the north there was the Antonine Wall, of earth, across the isthmus from the Firth of Forth to the Clyde. One must not think of Hadrian's Wall in simple terms at all; it was the central feature of an entire frontier area, of which innumerable relics remain. It was to Roman Britain what the North-West Frontier was to the British Empire in India, or the Chinese Wall to that largest of human civilizations.

Hadrian's Wall is complex enough in itself, with its forts at intervals, such as Chesters or Housesteads, presented to the nation not long ago by one of its most loyal historians, George Macaulay Trevelyan. Every mile there was a mile-castle, capable of holding fifty men. At a base-station like Corbridge one can peer into the lives of those vanished legionaries – as an imaginative writer like Kipling did: there are their quarters, granaries, storehouses; military offices, dormitories, bath-houses, latrines; dwelling-houses with typical Roman floor-heating such as was not to be witnessed again until our time. Masses of pottery and coins have come up from this rich soil – Caistor ware from the Midlands, red Samian from the Continent; altars, inscriptions, sculptures such as the famous Corbridge Lion, a work of forceful personal art.

Above A jug and a glass ribbed bowl from Radnage, Buckinghamshire. They both date from the first century A.D.

Right A hypocaust, or early form of central heating, in the Roman villa at Chedworth, Gloucestershire. Hypocausts carried hot air through ducts from a central furnace to warm the water in the baths, and to provide under-floor heating for the houses.

Left Hadrian's Wall, the line of Roman fortifications defending the northern frontier of Britain, was begun in AD 122 by the Roman Emperor of that name. It stretches for 73 miles across the north of England from Wallsend on the Tyne to Bowness on the Solway.

Hadrian's Wall served not only military but administrative and financial purposes. It controlled trade and the customs upon trade, the ingress of tribesmen into and egress out of the province. There was a communication road behind it, the Stanegate, an earthwork behind that, and roads leading to and from it. It was so strong that it never fell before a frontal attack: it was only when the garrisons were withdrawn that its functions ceased. Some early destruction wrought upon its foundations expressed the wild tribes' hatred of civilization. But the evidences remain: fragmentary shrines and altars to the deities worshipped, Celtic and Roman, local and cosmopolitan; innumerable monuments with their inscriptions to tell us the names and station of the dead who once served there. Many of these are collected in museums, like those at Edinburgh, Newcastle, York, Carlisle – which reminds us that the local museums all over the country contain treasures continually coming up from the earth.

Poussin once took up a handful of Roman earth; there filtered through his fingers fragments of coloured marbles and mosaics: *'C'est la poussière de Rome.'* ('It is the dust of Rome.') Few soils are as rich as the unrifled soil of Britain in the treasures that keep coming up: prehistoric gold torques, hoards of silver like those from Mildenhall or Traprain Law, enamels and jewellery, bronzes and sculptures, while mosaic floors not infrequently appear from under green fields. It is only in recent years that a very grand palace has been partly uncovered at Fishbourne, near Chichester: it covered many acres, most of it still buried under a huddle of council-houses. It was the residence of a tributary king, Cogidubnus – and a very good time he obviously had of it for his sensible submission to the empire. We today can enjoy his inheritance. He had the taste to be a patron of works of art: these have long lives, their makers short ones and they are remembered only by what they have left.

The Romano–British contribution to the artistic heritage of Britain is a rich and idiosyncratic one, widely varied in character as in quality. The sudden apparition of Roman architecture must have astonished the native inhabitants. The conquerors brought crafts

Early artistic influences: The Romans brought crafts such as mosaic, frescoes, and sculpture to Britain, and were able to render realistic natural forms to great effect, such as this leopard and tree, a detail from the Roman pavement at Woodchester in Gloucestershire.

Early Celtic art was given to abstract forms, as expressed in the circular design of this shield from Wales, dating from the late Bronze Age, 700–600 BC.

A medieval gravestone at Kilmarin, Argyll in Scotland, with its ancient Celtic symbols.

hitherto unknown – monumental carving, mosaics, frescoes and central heating. A simple distinction may be made between the capacity of civilized art to render realistic natural forms, especially the human figure, and the barbaric incapacity, the preference for abstract design and line.

Characteristic of Celtic art, as of the Celtic spirit in general, is a certain rejection of the real world, a withdrawal into a fantasy realm – one sees it in the lives of the early saints and hermits, as in the writing and art. Hence the visionary genius, the sensitiveness to line and coil and spiral. Marvels of their lesser art remain in their decorative work on cups and bronzes, such mirrors as those from Desborough or St Keverne. The natives learned from the Romans, but their inner inspiration is revealed in the long mournful heads of abstracted appearance which they sculpted. Both impulses continued long: the Roman in the church architecture of the Anglo-Saxons when they came to it, if falteringly. The Celtic had the more continuous vitality: the patterns of Roman mosaics, in their brilliant colours reappear in later manuscript illumination, and in fusion with the Anglo-Saxons' designs in the elaborate interlacing of the early crosses, along the lines where the impulses met and impregnated each other. All these early works – the famous Medusa head from Bath is an excellent example – blazed with colour once, like the temples and sculpture of Greece.

The undying legacy of the Roman presence in Britain was Christianity. It reached the island early, perhaps not long after AD 100, and had its first martyr in Alban of Verulam. The fact that it was an exclusive religion gave it a power which the tolerant and promiscuous pagan cults did not possess. A religion originally of towns and peasantry, it worked its passage upwards socially. In many cult-relics that remain we still see the mixture of pagan and Christian motifs and beliefs. The dynamism of Christianity had the force to expand and win. The Briton Patrick was the effective missionary of the faith to Ireland, which enjoyed a golden spell in insular security, until the eruption of the Vikings devastated northern Europe. And in the figure of Pelagius, British Christianity made a contribution of the first importance to the intellectual life of Europe. He had an unorthodox disbelief in the morose doctrine of original sin, and held firmly that men enjoyed a certain freedom of the will to shape their own lives, and hence a measure of moral responsibility. A perhaps continuous British inflexion may be observed in this; but it was too refined a view for the Dark Ages that ensued. It was a pity that the vehement psychology of the African Augustine (who believed in original sin and bondage of the will) had to prevail, laying emphasis on the brutal and violent nature of men.

THIS BECAME all too evident with the explosions from the German world – *furor Teutonicus* – which ruined the Roman Empire and fragmented civilization. One aspect of this immense, almost geological, movement was the Anglo-Saxon conquest of the half of Britain which is now known as England. This, more than anything else, affected the roots of the English people, and made them what they are. Where invasions before and after were apt to be of smaller groups, the incursions of Angles, Saxons and Jutes were movements of peoples. They left the mud-flats of the North Sea coast-line from Frisia to Jutland, rather deserted – according to Bede – for the more desirable lands of the inviting island.

This detail of St Cuthbert's coffin, now in Durham Cathedral, was made in the year 698. St Cuthbert was Bishop of Lindisfarne.

Even before the withdrawal of the Roman legions the province had been under attack all round the rim: from Irish, Scots and Picts in west and north, from Angles, Saxons and Jutes in the south-east. The fifth century is one of conflict and confusion, hence the darkness lit by such feeble glimmers as from Gildas, more concerned to lament than to tell us what happened – though it is thought now that his emphasis upon plague is one clue to the defeat of the Britons (disunity among the Celts may be another). Nor was the conquest, in one sense, ever entire. The English triumphs were to drive wedges across Britain to reach the western coasts at the Dee estuary and the Bristol Channel, thus splitting up the British areas from any unity or future integration. That lay henceforth with the English, with their better capacity for organization.

A long struggle waged to and fro, with a prolonged pause of half a century, which seems to have been won by a leader known traditionally as Arthur – it is difficult otherwise to account for the extraordinary force and tenacity of his legend. A victory at Mount Badon seems to be historical, and imposed a pause in which there must have been fertile interchange and contact, perhaps especially in the south-west, where the founder of the Wessex dynasty, Cerdic, has a Celtic name (Ceredig).

Evidences of the early pagan period of the English Conquest remain not only in their cemeteries with their grave-goods (some of it loot), but in the names of the days of the week: Tuesday, after the war-god, Tiw; Wednesday, after Woden, a kind of Jove, top-god; Thursday, from the god of thunder, Thunor; Friday, from the fertility goddess Frig. Even sacred Easter is named after a heathen goddess.

The Britons took no interest in converting their enemies – why should they? Characteristically they withdrew into their own world of religious experience, which we must not underestimate, for its evidences are all over the West. If one turns the map of Europe around on its side one can appreciate more easily that its western edge forms a world of its own traversed by its waterways – easier means of communication than by land.

Thus there was much movement – continuously from prehistoric times – between Ireland and Scotland, Wales, Cornwall, Brittany. Trade, traffic, religion, folk-lore, legend followed these routes. Numerous saints crossed the narrow Bristol Channel from Wales to Cornwall and Brittany, leaving their names and dedications of churches, their shrines, holy wells, and crosses across the land. The Roman memory is feebly carried forward in the monuments and inscriptions of the Dark Age – such as the 'Tristan' stone near Fowey: *Drustanus fili Cunomori*. Nor is it surprising that legends of Tristan and King Mark, Iseult and Gawen, should have been carried on further into the literature of the Middle Ages. Something of them goes back to the early written folk-tales of the Welsh, incorporated in the Mabinogion.

The conversion of the southern English came, however, from Rome with Augustine in 597. The perennial inspiration of Rome is expressed in the organization of the Anglo-Saxon church, and its special affiliation to Rome; the visits to Rome of early kings, payments of grateful tribute, Peter's Pence. (The word 'penny' comes down from those early times.) The influence may be *seen* strongly in Anglo-Saxon manuscripts, for example, the latinized script of the great *Codex Amiatinus* (an early manuscript in book form), taken as a present to the Pope.

The other side is the Celtic contribution to the creative Anglo-Celtic fusion – this time

Right A page from the superbly illustrated Lindisfarne Gospels, written around the year 700.

from the north, completing the cycle. As Patrick had converted Ireland to Christianity, thence came Columba to the fabulous missionary centre of Iona to convert and civilize the north: Galloway, under Ninian, near at hand; Northumbria, with Aidan, the leading Anglian kingdom which then ran from the Forth to the Humber, with its marvellous outpost at Lindisfarne. This sanctuary produced such creative works as the *Lindisfarne Gospels*, written and illuminated there around 700 – perhaps the finest ever executed in the island, comparable to that supreme Celtic masterpiece, the *Book of Kells*. The English Chad, trained by the northern Celts, missionized the Midlands, where he founded Lichfield, and Essex, where he built a church in the old Roman fort upon the Blackwater. It was an Irish monk who founded Malmesbury, while the Welsh St David added a chapel to Glastonbury, of ancient and misty memories.

A large number of sculpted crosses still remain in the north to testify to the fertilizing impulse of this fusion of cultures. Of such are those masterpieces, the Bewcastle and Ruthwell crosses – the latter, near Dumfries, deliberately defaced by order of the nefarious Scottish Assembly of 1642, so that two of its arms are missing.

The Reformation wrought untold damage to sculpture in Britain, which never really fully recovered; nor did religious painting. The losses in England were fearful, and were carried further by seventeenth-century Puritans in the Civil War. In Scotland the losses were irreparable: most of the abbeys and cathedrals, all the sculpture and painting, the whole series of the medieval tombs of the Scottish kings at Scone.

The sudden flowering of the early Anglo-Saxon achievement, from about 650 to 800, influenced the development of western Europe. This is brought home to us in the work of two of the three greatest of early Englishmen, Bede (673–735) and Boniface (680–755). Their work is still part of the continuous living tradition, made possible during a blissful interval of comparative security. Bede, in his monastic eyrie at Jarrow – Roman relics all round him, the well in the courtyard, the Wall at hand – was the greatest scholar in Europe: nothing quite parallel to him. We owe to him the classic account of the old English people, their coming to Britain and the progress of their conquest and colonization. In addition to works of Biblical scholarship, we largely owe him even our present system of dating and chronology.

Bede was a Northumbrian, Boniface (Winfrid) was a Wessex man, born in Devon. His life's work lay among his kin in Germany, where he not only missionized but carried through the organization of the Church, under the direction of Rome. His mission was an astonishing achievement; to this day the pastoral letters of the German episcopate are dated from his grave, as one hears them read in the churches: *'am Graben des heiligen Bonifazius'* ('from the grave of holy Boniface'). A large number of eminent Anglo-Saxons were involved in the good work: Willibrord in Frisia became patron saint of Utrecht; Willehad, bishop of Bremen, missionized the Danish borderlands. Many of his companions were massacred by their Saxon cousins, as Boniface was ultimately martyred with fifty of his mission in Frisia.

A distinctive feature of the work was the part played in it by holy women. A more continuing influence was that of Anglo-Saxon learning. The *Frankish Annals* followed English models; the *Anglo-Saxon Chronicle* itself is unique. This reminds us that their literature is probably the richest legacy of the Old English to posterity: no other of the Germanic peoples has anything to compare with it so early. This is curious, and is a significant pointer to the remote future; for literature was to become the chief English contribution to the arts: words, rather than music (as with the Germans), or visual art (as with the Latins).

The primacy of Northumbria was succeeded by that of the middle kingdom of Mercia, especially under a notable king, Offa. We still remember him by Offa's Dyke, the remarkable earthwork which he raised as a boundary between his kingdom and Wales. Offa is memorable too for his fine coins, a type which persisted right into the Middle Ages: the continuous history of the English currency goes right back to Offa. The Old Irish called their coin, *oiffing*, after him.

The career of the last of the trinity of great Englishmen, Alfred of Wessex (849–899), fell in the appalling time of the Viking invasions. In the event these invasions practically destroyed Old English civilization. The Scandinavian eruption affected most of northern Europe, but chiefly the British Isles. Here it took two forms: the mainly Danish attacks on England, and the Norse campaigns all round the northern coasts, Scotland, Ireland, the Isle of Man – even in the Bristol Channel they have left their names. Their contribution to the population is important, even though they did not contribute much in other ways. In 793 they plundered and destroyed defenceless Lindisfarne, Bede's Jarrow the following year. From that they went on, with varying pauses, but did not wholly cease until they conquered the kingship (at least) with Canute – a prelude to the ultimate Norman Conquest, by the descendants of these people from their French colony across the Channel.

Sculpted crosses testify to the influence of missionary work from Ireland in Britain, like this one at Bewcastle in Cumberland.

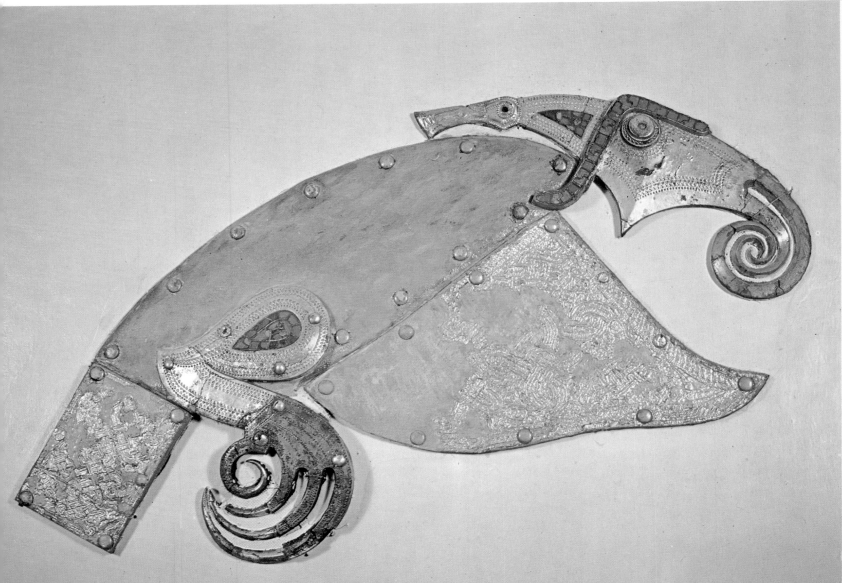

The Danes found Britain good for living in, as had their Anglian cousins before them – now their victims; neither of them could ever 'have had it so good' where they came from. In the upshot considerable settlements of Norse stock were made all round from Shetlands and Orkney to the Hebrides, thence around the Irish coasts, and from there to the Isle of Man and Cumbria, whose population is mixed Celtic-Anglian–Norse. The Danes settled in larger numbers all down the eastern coast of England from Northumbria to East Anglia – most heavily in Yorkshire, but also southward in the East Midlands, the counties that constituted the Danelaw. One can *see* their presence in place-names ending with -by, -thorpe, and -thwaite, alongside Anglian -ham, or -ton; for both types of conquering colonizers came to rest upon British soil, cheek by jowl with each other.

The Vikings owed their prodigious success to their shipbuilding and skill in navigation: they were wonderful navigators, besides possessing the initiative, and surprising flexibility of

The Alfred Jewel, belonging to Alfred the Great, ninth-century Wessex king. It bears the inscription 'Alfred had me made'. Made of rock-crystal over enamel set in gold, it shows the beautiful workmanship of which the Saxons were capable.

28

Above This eighth-century picture stone shows a Viking ship, with its customary high prow and square sail.

movement, that that gave them. One cannot give them high marks for any cultural contribution, but they must have contributed to historic, if remoter, maritime enterprise. Captain Cook of the Pacific, historic navigator, was born upon their coast, near Whitby; Nelson was born at a thorpe, Burnham Thorpe in Norfolk.

Alfred's grandfather had won primacy for Wessex by subduing the Celtic south-west, and a process of natural integration seems to have gone forward there: though Britons were expelled from Exeter, the dedications of a number of the churches remained Celtic. The first Danish raid was upon Wessex, and it fell to her to organize something like a national defence. Alfred was the first to achieve this, when the co-ordination of Danish attacks threatened England as a nation. He created a fleet and, against natural English inertia, called into being an operative nationwide militia. Most of his life was spent in fighting off attacks, warding off danger. Although he is such a hero to the English, and rightly so, one must recognize that he succeeded in saving only one-half, or perhaps two-thirds, of England – all that south of old Watling Street.

Alfred did indeed fight the Danes to a standstill, imposed a peace and the acceptance of Christianity, conceding the Danelaw, with its noticeable number of free men and its particular customs and institutions. The 'ridings' and 'wapentakes' of Yorkshire are Scandinavian words, and perhaps the breezy brusqueness of Yorkshiremen and the toughness of Eastern Englanders bespeak their origins.

After Alfred had imposed a truce upon the invaders, after all the raids, the pursuits across the face of the land, he had a ravaged country to repair. All was to do again: he had to set on foot the re-education of his people, restore learning and culture. To this end he set himself to learn, so that he could teach. He thought nothing worse in men than 'not to know': that in itself makes him live for us, a real father of his country. He had to call in help now from the Continent, as from the Celts: Asser, a priest from St David's, whom he made bishop of Sherborne, became his friend and wrote his biography with affection.

Sir Alec Clifton-Taylor sums up this most appealing character among all English kings.

On any estimate, he was the most effective ruler who had appeared in Western Europe since the death of Charlemagne. But beneath his preoccupation with duties, often of desperate urgency, there was always a sense of imponderable values. No other king of the Dark Ages ever set himself, like ·Alfred, to explore whatever in the literature of Christian antiquity might explain the problems of fate and free will ... and the ways by which a man comes to knowledge. His unique importance in the history of English letters comes from his conviction that a life without knowledge or reflection was unworthy of respect, and his determination to bring the thought of the past within the range of his subjects' understanding. The translations of ancient books by which he tried to reach this end form the beginning of English prose literature.

Across the ages we recognize an admirable spirit.

FOR ALL THAT, things were never the same with Anglo-Saxon England. Something seems to have broken under the strain. Ethelred the Unready, as the school-books call him, was a kind of Neville Chamberlain of the tenth century; the correct soubriquet is 'Redeless', i.e. without counsel.

Thus the country lost the sense of integration for which Alfred had fought so hard. He had recovered Mercian London from the Danes – a master-key to the country; while his coins called him *Rex Saxonum*, King of all the Saxons. The Anglo-Saxon revival of the tenth century was essentially a church affair, impelled by such remarkable men as Dunstan from Glastonbury and Ethelwold from Winchester. There is still visible evidence in manuscript illumination of the Winchester School – of which the Benedictional of St Ethelwold is a masterpiece. Actually these manuscripts were being made in various monastic centres, from Canterbury to Sherborne, while the fullest collection of Anglo-Saxon poetry remains in Leofric's book from Exeter.

Towards the end of the Old England, Canute's conquest made it a province of an empire across the North Sea – though geography determined that the future would not lie that way. Edward the Confessor, last king of the Old English house, was half a Norman; the latter half of his reign was dominated by the House of Godwin, which was Scandinavian – Harold, 'the last of the Saxons', was not a Saxon. The scene was set for the conquest from across the Channel; William the Conqueror regarded himself as the heir of the Confessor, who was too holy to have children (or, perhaps, was incapable of it). But it was the military technique of the Normans that won at Hastings – as with the Panzer divisions of the Germans in 1940. After that the superior military organization, the will-power and initiative of the Normans closed Britain to further invasion. Scandinavian incursions were ended for good and all; the future of England was to lie properly with the Continent, first and foremost with France, from which superior civilization came – not from the German world.

There went along with this the administrative genius of the Normans. They inherited a great deal from the Old England, notably a centralized treasury at Winchester and a national system of taxation; but the Normans welded an inefficient state apparatus into a strong, forceful and expansionist state. Internally, the famous monument to its efficiency is *Domesday Book*: no other country has such a complete early survey of its resources, such a map of its social system and how it operated.

The Anglo-Saxons were defeated and hammered, the top of their society decapitated. But the Normans were few in number, a military aristocracy, French in language and manners, which formed the governing class over the next few centuries. The English – or, rather, the Anglo-Celtic people beneath – continued, the dominant element being English, as the language witnesses. It is a theme of this book that submerged elements keep emerging as shifts and class-changes occur in society. So the language continued, though it was to undergo transformation and an enormous enrichment from its more civilized Romance contacts. Even simple differences illustrate changes in society.

Above A detail from the Bayeux Tapestry, showing the death of King Harold at the Battle of Hastings in 1066. The tradition of Harold being killed by an arrow in the eye stems from this illustration (see the figure beneath the word 'Harold').

Right The Norman soldiers foraged in the English countryside for food and provisions. This detail from the Bayeux Tapestry shows how the Saxon peasants suffered.

30

REX : INTERFEC TVS : EST

ENTVR : HIC : EST : VVAD ARD :

odie si uocem eius audieritis : no
e obdurare corda uestra.
sicut in irritacione : secundum die

Old English words, like ox, sheep, calf, swine, deer, indicate that submerged Saxons had the care of the animals, which, when eaten by their Norman masters, became beef, mutton, veal, pork and bacon, venison. Similarly revealing of the new social structure was the fact that French words came in for master and servant; bottle, buttery and butler; dinner, supper, and banquet. Most of our words relating to government and administration, law and property, came in with the Normans.

Anglo-Saxon poetry continued, to surface with Langland's *Piers the Ploughman*, significantly enough towards 1400, when French was losing its ascendancy. When English came uppermost again with Chaucer, Langland and Gower, it was not the literary Anglo-Saxon of before the Conquest, or of the Anglo-Saxon Chronicle which was continued after it. That sank into the dialect of Somerset and Dorset, which represents it. The language in which the poetry of Caedmon was written and which Bede spoke lapsed into North Country dialect – Northumbrian and Lowland Scots. It was the language of the Midlands – Anglian not Saxon – which was to prevail, and that was Mercian. London was a Mercian town, and its key

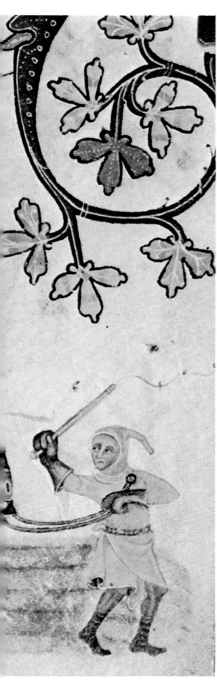

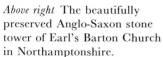 *Above right* The beautifully preserved Anglo-Saxon stone tower of Earl's Barton Church in Northamptonshire.

importance is again revealed in the part it had in making Mercian our speech, instead of the southern and northern lingo, which had much more literature to show. London was essentially commercial, and commerce counts. It is amusing to think that, all over the English-speaking world today, across the North American and Australian continents, from Canada and the Middle West to New Zealand, people are speaking Mercian, and are unaware of it.

2 CAPITALS AND REGIONAL CENTRES

THE MOST STRIKING VISIBLE EVIDENCE of the Norman Conquest is the Tower of London, the square White Tower built by William to protect, and also fortify his hold upon, the richest commercial centre in the country. Commerce was the essence of its being: it was never the governmental capital. That remained for some three hundred years – from the time of Alfred to the Conqueror's nephew, Stephen – at Winchester. Alfred had refounded it as the largest of his fortified *burhs*; today evidences of that early period are coming up from the soil around the cathedral, including the complete foundations of the early Saxon minster. For the finest Anglo-Saxon church remaining we must go to the basilica at Brixworth – even so, truncated of aisles and portico; and for a fine tower, to Earl's Barton: both in Northamptonshire.

The Normans signalized their rule at Winchester with characteristic will-power and energy by pulling down a section of the town (as in many other places – Oxford, for example) to build a castle, then building a new cathedral and a new royal palace. The basic pattern of streets of Alfred's capital still survives. The treasury of the realm remained here until the anarchy of Stephen's reign, when Winchester lost its primacy to Westminster, which became henceforth the capital.

Evidences of the heyday of Winchester remain in the Norman parts of the cathedral, the fresco preserved in the Holy Sepulchre Chapel, the famous illuminated Bible, and the embroideries which formed the *genre* of Anglo-Saxon art most admired on the Continent (along with its metal-work). The Bayeux Tapestry itself, which records the genesis and events of the Conquest, is sometimes thought to be of English workmanship; English needlework, stitchwork and embroidery, remained a speciality all through the Middle Ages. A surprising amount of this legacy remains, such as the superb chasuble in red and gold, with its winged angels and leopards, from the fourteenth century, in the Metropolitan Museum, New York.

An endearing reminder of Anglo-Saxon Winchester is that of its early bishop, St Swithun. The body of this holy man was moved to the old cathedral on 15 July 971. In country places all over southern England people still think that, if it rains on St Swithun's day, it will rain for the forty following days: no amount of meteorological evidence to the contrary persuaded popular belief. It is interesting, however, to think of folklore as a continuing part of a people's heritage.

London is such a world in itself that it is difficult for the English to grasp it as a unity. This is not surprising, as many eminent foreign observers consider that London's special character is due precisely to its disunity, its spontaneity and the naturalness of its growth. The Dane Rasmussen describes it as a 'scattered city', as opposed to the concentrated capitals of the Continent reflecting the dominance of absolute monarchies. The leading American authority on cities, Lewis Mumford, pays tribute to it as 'the most decentralized and individualized of all great cities, the one most capable of maintaining the human scale . . . its brick and stone interwoven with constant patches of green in its parks and squares, and with endless areas of concealed back-yard gardens.' He considers that something of this priceless character is being thrown away in the ill-considered thronging of high-rise buildings. Contrast the beauty of Canaletto's views of London in the eighteenth century when all was in proportion, Wren's steeples rising above the buildings like the forest of masts in the port of London; all presided over by the controlled majesty of his St Paul's.

London from these early times was two cities: the commercial City within its wall; and Westminster, where the chief royal residence lay, and hence the seat of executive government, in the shadow of the Confessor's Abbey, rebuilt in French style by Henry III, a keen connoisseur of the arts. The Houses of Parliament are still styled after the royal residence, the Palace of Westminster. In the Tudor period the monarchs came to reside at Whitehall near by, where a complex of buildings arose, the most notable of which remains: Inigo Jones's Renaissance Banqueting Hall. Thus developed in time a mass of governmental and

Previous pages The Tower of London and Tower Bridge. In the centre is the White Tower, the oldest part.

Westminster Abbey, founded by Edward the Confessor, was rebuilt by Henry III. Every king and queen of England has been crowned here since William the Conqueror in 1066.

Middle Temple Hall at the Inns of Court,
London.

administrative buildings, from Admiralty Arch and Trafalgar Square to the Thames. Of these, architecturally, William Kent's Horse Guards is worthy of the eighteenth century in which it was built.

Most of the operative London of history lies along the north bank of the Thames. On the south bank is Lambeth Palace, official residence of the primates of the English Church, the archbishops of Canterbury. Opposite historic London Bridge, Southwark was a 'liberty' of its own, with a large church which is now a cathedral. Close by was the Elizabethan theatre area of Shakespeare's Globe, Henslowe's Rose and Fortune; it is appropriate that the Festival Hall and National Theatre continue the festive tradition of Bankside.

On the north bank Westminster came to connect up with London along the Strand, where the names of streets commemorate the mansions of Elizabethan nobles (Essex and Norfolk Streets), or earlier settlements are remembered in the parish church of St Clement *Danes*, or the medieval Savoy, or again, in the City, Lombard Street. The most beautiful of London's palaces, Somerset House, masterpiece of Sir William Chambers, here dominates the river frontage. Thence eastwards one might describe as the law capital of the realm, for it is occupied by the courts and gardens of the Temple and Middle Temple, Inns of Court. Lincoln's Inn and Gray's Inn lie farther north, while along the present Strand lies the Victorian Gothic masterpiece, the Law Courts. East of that, along Fleet Street, is the newspaper capital of the country.

This book cannot be an architectural anthology: one can only cite representatively what helps to reveal the country's historic legacy. Thus the splendid late seventeenth-century squares of Westminster, like St James's, the eighteenth-century squares of Bloomsbury – of which Bedford Square remains complete and undamaged – and the nineteenth-century

Above Whitehall seen from St James's Park.

Above The porch of St Pancras Church in London.

Left The West front of St Paul's Cathedral. Old St Paul's was destroyed by the Great Fire of London in 1666. Sir Christopher Wren spent 36 years of his life achieving the magnificent classical cathedral we know today.

squares of Kensington and Belgravia demonstrate before our eyes the concentration and taste, and the progressive expansion, of the English governing class. In their heyday – from the Elizabethan Age to the First World War – the British governing class ruled more successfully than any other in Europe; to it we owe the marvellous expansion which carried the English language all over the world and made it, in effect, the first world-language.

Rasmussen and Mumford make a great deal of the openness of London, the green spaces of Hyde Park, Regent's Park and Hampstead Heath, along with numerous smaller parks, like St James's, let alone the big gardens of such as Berkeley and Grosvenor Squares (in New York these would be designated 'parks'). Rasmussen observes how the growth of London reflects the nature of English society, free and flexible, with its individualism and spontaneity. It may not equal Paris, Rome or New York as spectacle, but none of these has sufficient open spaces. The absolute French monarchy, followed by Napoleonic imperialism, imposed regularity and magnificence upon Paris, to some detriment of civic life.

This was impossible in London, where the City was a power of its own. At several junctures its power was decisive: in supporting the Yorkists for the throne, against the incompetent government of the legitimate king, Henry VI; again in its support of Parliament against Charles I – it was London that really won the Civil War – and, when the City found that the country could not be run without monarchy, in bringing about the Restoration.

The comparative smallness of the royal palaces in London tells the same story: no Versailles or Louvre, no Hofburg or royal palace like that in Madrid. (Windsor is a different story, but it has always served several purposes.) The palaces of leading aristocrats, notably after the Revolution of 1688, were larger: Chatsworth of the Cavendishes, Blenheim of the Churchills, Boughton of the Montagus, Holkham, Trentham, Eaton Hall. St James's was never very large, though it has lost a wing; Buckingham Palace was not big until Edward VII put on an opulent front. The residential areas themselves reveal the wealth and taste of the aristocracy. The beautiful squares of Bloomsbury – today in bits and pieces – testified to the aesthetic control exercised by the Dukes of Bedford, as did the collections in their palace at Woburn. Rasmussen pays tribute to the imagination that went into the development of the Marylebone estate; we may add to these the Victorian planning of Belgravia under the Grosvenors, carried out largely by a builder of genius, Thomas Cubitt.

The grand piece of royal planning was that promoted by the connoisseur Regent and his architect, Nash: the linking of St James's Park to Regent's Park through Piccadilly, Regent Street and Portland Place, to the splendid terraces, columned and porticoed, colour-washed and elegant, around the green spaces of Regent's Park, with its lake and zoo. The expansive energy and prosperity of the Elizabethans meant that they began filling in the gardens and open spaces of the City proper. Beyond the wall were the clear spaces favoured for their exercises, archery, artillery, musters: Moorfields and Mile End, as we remember from Justice Shallow's reminiscences. At one time Milton lived in 'a pretty garden-house' giving on to St James's Park; at another he resided in Artillery Walk, Bunhill Fields – 'like all Milton's houses it had a garden'. John Bunyan is buried in the famous Nonconformist cemetery in Bunhill Fields. The earliest Elizabethan theatres were out in the fields of Shoreditch, the parish in which many of the theatre folk and foreign musicians lived – Shakespeare's musical Dark Lady, Emilia Bassano, was the daughter of one of them.

One of Britain's most visible contributions to the world has been the steam-locomotive and the railway: perhaps the Railway Age was its heyday. Just as London was the hub of the Roman road-system, so the network of the nation's railways pivoted upon it. The memorials of that age of energy remain: St Pancras Station, with the long curve of its rooflines, and the Hotel, turreted and fantasticated, clamorous and imaginative as the Victorian Age itself. Euston had a more monumental approach: grand columns and pedimented portico used to herald the 'gateway to the North'. King's Cross has a sober and distinguished front; all the big railway-halls bespeak the imagination and expertise of the Industrial Revolution iron industry, its arts and crafts.

Again, London's underground railway system was the first in the world. Here we may pay tribute to the optimum it achieved in the 1930s, with Charles Holden as the architect of genius who carried out the formulation of their designs. One recognizes his hand in the elegant little stations, above and below ground, the shapely proportions, nothing thrown away; and in the big Underground Railway Building in St James's, that masterpiece of the 1930s.

Nor should one forget the vast complex of docks, wharves, warehouses, which made London for long the first port in Europe. The Thames is the main artery of London, and was even more so in earlier centuries when movement by water was easier than by land. The Elizabethan wherries were the taxis of those days; the wherrymen's cries of 'Westward ho!' and 'Eastward ho!' have come down in the tradition somewhat unrecognizably, one as a Jacobean play, the other as a Victorian novel.

What are the images that London conjures up in the mind?

Up to the Great Fire of 1666 the dominant image would undoubtedly have been that of Old St Paul's, followed by London Bridge. Old St Paul's was one of the grandest churches of Christendom, considerably longer than Wren's and with a spire that ran up a hundred feet higher: a monument to the religious ardour, the wealth and civic pride of its medieval merchant classes. We know very well what it looked like, inside and out, from the splendid engravings of Hollar; and also from drawings, views of the city by Wyngaerde, Visscher and others. The huge church drew itself up proudly above the huddle of buildings (no less than 130 churches, of which few – such as part of St Bartholomew's, Smithgate and Shakespeare's St Helen's, Bishopsgate – remain). At the beginning of Elizabeth's reign St Paul's lost its lofty spire by lightning, so the views show the central tower truncated. The vast nave was much used for sheltered business – Paul's Walk. The tidy soul of Archbishop Laud did not approve of this secularity: he inspired Inigo Jones's enormous portico, the grandest of its kind in Europe except for St Peter's.

Old London Bridge is familiar too, crowded as it was with tall houses, and with the narrow archways which made 'shooting the bridge' a dangerous business at certain states of the tide. One sees the bridge in many pictures and engravings, notably in Samuel Scott's paintings of it. It has entered into folklore, the unconscious mental life of the people, in the nursery rhyme:

> *London Bridge is broken down, broken down,*
> *My fair lady!*

An encyclopaedia of its own would be needed to express what London has stood for in the intellectual and artistic life of the nation, let alone the historic, political and social, economic and financial. Portraying various aspects of the city has inspired many artists, from those earlier ones to Turner and Constable, with his exquisite views from Hampstead away over

A detail from Jan Visscher's panoramic map of London, 1650. On the north side of the river can be seen 'Old St Paul's', built during the fourteenth century, towering above the city. On the other side of the river and just to the right is Shakespeare's Globe Theatre; to the left of the theatre is the Bear Garden. The original London Bridge is also shown.

the city; and so on to fascinated foreigners, Monet, Sisley and Tissot, and the naturalized Whistler and Sickert. London has been put into music by Elgar and Vaughan Williams, and given its name to a symphony of Haydn.

In literature its inspiration has been legion, all the way from William Dunbar to Eliot's *The Waste Land.* Everyone knows Dunbar's:

> *London, thou art of townès A per se.*
> *Sovereign of cities, seemliest in sight,*
> *Of high renown, riches and royalty;*
> *Of lordes, barons, and many a goodly knight;*
> *Of most delectable lusty ladies bright;*
> *Of famous prelatès, in habitès clerical;*
> *Of merchants full of substance and of might:*
> *London, thou art the flower of cities all.*

A generous tribute from a Scot. The fifteenth-century ballad 'London Lickpenny' takes us into its life more vividly. 'Some call London a lickpenny,' we are told, 'because of feastings and other occasions of expense.'

> *Then I hied me into East Cheap:*
> *One cries, 'Ribs of beef and many a pie!'*
> *Pewter pots they clattered on a heap;*
> *There was harp, pipe, and minstrelsy.*
> *'Yea, by cock!', 'Nay, by cock!' some began cry;*
> *Some sang of Jenkin and Julian for their meed* [reward],
> *But for lack of money I might not speed.*

Another view of London Bridge by Samuel Scott, at Felbrigg House in Norfolk. The original London Bridge was begun in 1176 and finished in 1209. It was not until 1825 that the present bridge was begun.

It is the world of Shakespeare's scenes at the Boar's Head in Cheapside; or of Ben Jonson's *Bartholomew Fair*; or, with a different inflexion, of Beaumont's Letter to Ben:

> *What things have we seen*
> *Done at the Mermaid! heard words that have been*
> *So nimble, and so full of subtle flame*
> *As if that every one from whence they came*
> *Had meant to put his whole wit in a jest.*

Milton's life was a London life, born and bred and buried there – evidences of it occur all through his work, not only specific sonnets such as 'When the Assault was intended to the City'. Pepys's Diary gives us an immensely more appealing picture of a London life; Evelyn's is busy and evocative, but rather priggish – as he was. Dr Johnson became a confirmed Londoner, though his poem *London*, with which he first won fame, was more of a political tract than a depiction of life. That, however, is fully made up by Boswell's *Life* which fills in the London background of its lumbering literary bear, *Ursus major*, for us. That bulky ghost still lumbers round Fleet Street and Gough Square, and his parish church of St Clement Danes. His addiction became such that at last he was able to say, 'When a man is tired of London he is tired of life; for there is in London all that life can afford.'

The most vivid rendering of life in London is, of course, in the works of Dickens; after him, on rather different levels, come Trollope and Henry James. Thackeray did a lot of his writing not in his saddened Kensington home, but in the most literary of London clubs, with its fine library, the Athenaeum. (Matthew Arnold regarded its quiet as 'something resembling beatitude'.)

Henry James has described, with his usual indirection and self-analysis, his first acquaintance with Victorian London. 'No doubt I had the mystic prescience of how fond of the murky modern Babylon I was one day to become.' Victorian London was as smoky as a Rembrandt, lit by similar lurid glows, rich and exciting. The atmosphere is clearer today. But Henry James relished 'the thick, dim distances which in my opinion are the most romantic town-vistas in the world'. They were intensely stimulating to the novelist; he was in the habit of taking walks at night to watch what was going on in the teeming human aquarium. 'London is indeed an epitome of the round world.' He singles out the fantasy view that opens eastward from the Serpentine, and settles for the rusticity within the vast city, for example, 'from Notting Hill to Whitehall: you may traverse this immense distance altogether on soft, fine turf, amid the song of birds, the bleat of lambs, the ripple of ponds, the rustle of admirable trees'. He thought it 'a real stroke of luck for a particular country that the capital of the human race happens to be British', and went on, 'surely every other people would have it theirs if they could. . . . Whether the English deserve to hold it any longer might be an interesting field of inquiry.' The dubiety suggests – apparently not.

It is another American, T. S. Eliot, with his sensitive nose for death, decay and destruction, who has celebrated London in the most famous of modern poems:

> *London Bridge is falling down falling down falling down.*

Actually, he could not bear to live anywhere other than in London.

Once more the best evidence of what the place means in the unconscious life of the nation is in the nursery rhyme:

> *Pussy cat, pussy cat, where have you been?*
> *I've been up to London to see the queen.*

Edinburgh Castle was founded on Castle Rock in the twelfth century. Within its walls Mary Queen of Scots gave birth to the future King James VI of Scotland and I of England.

THE SECOND CAPITAL in the island is Edinburgh – of Anglian foundation as its name shows, while Glasgow is Celtic. That it is a true capital of a separate nation, an historian appreciates better than anyone; for Scotland has a very different character from England, a distinct history and tradition. The racial elements may not be so far apart, for Lowland Scots are Anglian by origin. But the mixture is different: the strong Celtic element, not confined to Gaelic Scots and Irish, is from the Northern Celts.

The history of Scotland has been in marked contrast, so too its social structure. The constitutional backbone of English history in modern times has been the alliance between a strong monarchy and the middle elements of society, country gentry and urban middle classes. This kept order in the nursery, and gave England a powerful integration other countries lacked; Scotland above all – geography helped largely to detract from it. A king was no more than a 'first among equals'. There was hardly any middle class; the aristocracy were much more powerful than in England. Such unity as the country achieved came through the Presbyterian Kirk.

45

Visually Edinburgh is the most striking and sharply etched city in this island – and indeed it has often been etched, it offers so good a subject. In the heyday of its cultural life in the late eighteenth century, Scots were proud to call their capital 'the Athens of the North': this could refer not only to its vivid intellectual life but to its romantic situation, between the mountain of Arthur's Seat hovering over Holyrood and the Firth of Forth always in the view, the port of Leith as its Piraeus. The strategic nub of the situation was the height at the end of the mile-long spine upon which the castle was built, with steep declivities on three sides, and in earlier times it frowned down into the waters of the Nor' Loch, now filled with gardens and monuments.

Along that windy ridge, from the castle down to Holyrood Abbey and its neighbouring royal palace, occurred many of the stirring events of Scottish history. The place is full of memories – of Mary Queen of Scots whose tragic story went all over Europe into its literature and art, poetry, drama, opera; of John Knox; and that most suggestive image of all, against a lighted window a hand racing across the page – the unknown author of *Waverley*, who created the historical novel and patented it in all the literatures of Europe.

The mountain of Arthur's Seat 'hovering' over Holyrood.

A view of the city of Edinburgh from Calton Hill. Edinburgh is the historic capital of Scotland, and lies in a magnificent setting close to the southern shore of the Firth of Forth.

The burgh was founded by Edwin, first Christian king of Northumbria; his line was succeeded by rulers from the Celtic kingdom of Dalriada, who welded together Scots (originally from Ireland, and the same people – so why should they quarrel?) with Picts and Anglians to make the Scottish kingdom. The earliest building to remain is the chapel of St Margaret within the Castle, a small parallel to the chapel of St John within the Tower of London. Through this sainted queen the Old English royal house continued in the Scottish line after the Normans had conquered England.

Holyrood Abbey stands there at the lower end of the 'Royal Mile', a roofless ruin, and only the nave at that: a silent monument to the destruction the Reformation wrought in Scotland, the withering blast that bit off the promising Renaissance buds of Scottish literature – the admirable Gavin Douglas, David Lindsay, and Robert Henrison who carried on the inspiration of the greatest of English medieval writers, Chaucer. (Nor must one forget the enduring inspiration to Arthurian literature of the brilliant prose writer, Malory.)

After the ghastly turmoils of the seventeenth century, with extremes making life dangerous for sensible people in the middle – after dour Covenanters and the Stuart deviations of the '15 and '45 Rebellions alike – rational persons came into their own and made a brilliantly gifted society in the decades before and after 1800. The most original of British philosophers with his profound scepticism, Hume; the admirable historian, Robertson; the first and most sensible of economists, Adam Smith; writers like Scott, Burns and James Hogg; painters like the exquisite Alan Ramsay and Raeburn, never surpassed for the rendering of character; architects of genius like Robert Adam, who designed some of the buildings of the New Town and the loveliest interiors of Scottish houses like Mellerstain and Culzean, as well as Sion, Osterley and Kenwood in London: all these expressed the latent genius of the Scottish people hitherto inhibited by Presbyterianism. The rational beauty of the Georgian New Town versus the Old may represent visually two sides of the Scottish historical experience.

The union with England enabled the excess energy of the Scots to pour itself into the south and outwards into the empire. The Scottish contribution to Canada has been a dominating one. The Scottish contribution to the British Empire in India – that marvellous episode in world-history – was hardly less notable; while Scots have been much to the fore in government at the centre – again one *sees* it in the names of Prime Ministers, Gladstone, Balfour, MacDonald, Macmillan – as again in education, especially university education.

Scotland is a real entity as a nation, her personality and history fascinating. What is happiest in the nationalist (or even provincial) impulse is to be seen in literature. Walter Scott's genius was a creative influence not only in English literature but in European (c.f. Victor Hugo, Tolstoy, Mazzoni) and American (witness Fenimore Cooper). The Scottish inflexion in literature is particularly appealing – in such a fine poet as Edwin Muir, from the Orkneys, or those descendants of Scott, Robert Louis Stevenson and John Buchan.

Stevenson, who came from a family of lighthouse builders, evokes the splendid tradition of that dangerous profession. One thinks of the lighthouses all round Britain's exposed coasts, from Dover's Roman pharos to the Eddystone (with which Winstanley, an earlier builder, perished) and on to the Bishop at the westernmost outpost of the Scillies; up the Irish Sea to Holyhead, looking across to Dublin, founded by the Vikings, and thence through the Hebrides around to Cape Wrath. From there to granite Aberdeen and down the eastern coasts, where now the hidden wealth of the latest Industrial Revolution – oil – is now coming ashore.

Stevenson paid tribute to all lighthouse builders and keepers in the person of his father:

And bright on the lone isle, the foundered reef,
The long resounding foreland, Pharos stands.
These are thy works, O father, these thy crown ...
I must arise, O father, and to port
Some lost, complaining seaman pilot home.

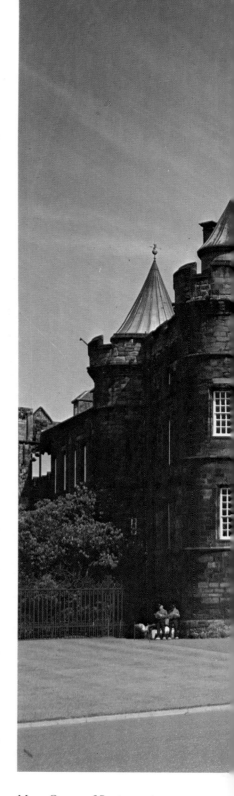

Mary Queen of Scots spent much of her troubled reign at Holyrood Palace. It was there that her second husband, Lord Darnley, murdered her favourite, David Riccio, before her eyes. Darnley was murdered in his turn and Mary was indirectly implicated in his death.

After Scott, Stevenson evoked Edinburgh best in his novels, and Scotland herself, in lines to a fellow Scots writer, from his last post in remote Samoa:

> *Be it granted me to behold you again in dying,*
> *Hills of home! and to hear again the call;*
> *Hear about the graves of the martyrs the peewees crying,*
> *And hear no more at all.*

Stevenson's writing had a creative influence in other arts: it inspired Vaughan Williams' song-cycle, *Songs of Travel*. While Housman's *A Shropshire Lad* inspired an even finer cycle, *On Wenlock Edge*; as well as songs and an orchestral suite by George Butterworth, one of the many men of talent to be massacred in the holocaust of the First World War.

Left Very little remains of the Norman Castle in Cardiff – much more of the 'castellated Victorian grandeur of the Marquises of Bute' is in evidence.

WALES – so like a Celtic country – lacks a centre and has never had a capital of its own. Besides that there was always a dichotomy, sometimes a ding-dong struggle, between north and south. In the Tudor heyday, when the Welsh gave the ablest dynasty to England, Wales was governed by a council under a lord president, from Shrewsbury and Ludlow. Shrewsbury Castle has the Old Council House opposite. Ludlow dominates the Teme; here, before the lord president, Milton's *Comus* was performed by the younger members of the family. Sir Philip Sidney's father was for long lord president, under Elizabeth, and built the range of which one sees the shell. The oak panelling in the Feathers Inn came from the castle. A more affecting memorial is the tablet to Philip Sidney's little sister, Ambrosia, in the church. At the foot of the tower outside lie the ashes of the poet Housman:

> *Leave your home behind you,*
> *Your friends by field and town:*
> *Oh, town and field will mind you*
> *Till Ludlow tower is down.*

Cardiff, which serves for a Welsh capital, is historically a frontier town. Its nature is revealed to the visitor by the grand rectangle that remains, the base of the Roman frontier station. Within are small bits of the medieval castle in one corner, but vastly more of the castellated Victorian grandeur of the Marquises of Bute. To the enterprise of this Scots family – Stuarts too! – Cardiff owes its growth; for they risked their fortune to begin the docks which brought the town, and them, prosperity and constituted a glory of the place. In balance to the docks is a remarkable example of early twentieth-century town-planning: the lay-out of Cathays Park. Here, along with City Hall, university and library, is the Welsh National Museum and Art Gallery, with its collections of Welsh antiquities, folk-life, and painting – works by such painters as Richard Wilson and Augustus John. For, with the deliquescence of Nonconformity in our time, the artistic impulses of the Welsh have been released into art and literature, with poets like Dylan Thomas and Vernon Watkins, or a remarkable novelist and short-story writer such as Rhys Davies.

WITHIN ENGLAND herself there has been through the ages a marked dichotomy between north and south, which has erupted in earlier wars, and still provides a strong contrast in personality and accent. Again and again the backward and obstinate north has been hammered – notably by Henry VIII in suppressing the Pilgrimage of Grace. Once more the north suffered heavily in the suppression of the Rising of the Northern Earls in 1569. In the Civil War the less enlightened north and west were defeated by the Parliamentarian (and Puritan) south and east pivoting upon London. Earlier, William the Conqueror utterly harried the north for its resistance: the devastation is recorded in *Domesday Book*.

Right An example of the remarkable twentieth century town-planning in Cardiff – the Civic Centre and City Hall.

Above York Minster, or the Cathedral of St Peter, built between the thirteenth and fifteenth centuries, towers above the city of York.

Left The Guildhall, York, was built between 1446 and 1448. Much of the arcade of wooden columns was gutted in the Second World War, but it has now been rebuilt. Here it is seen from across the River Ouse.

Right St William's College,
York, built in 1453, was
originally a college for priests.
In the foreground is the
seventeenth-century court.

The historic line of division comes at the Trent: York was the capital of the north. During the sixteenth century and up to the Civil War much of the north was governed by a council, with a lord president, which sat at York. No city more speaks of its historic past: it is a splendid *ville musée*, like 'Rouen. Everything is there – for as long as it may last.

Yorkshire, with its three large ridings, is more than a county. It resembles a small kingdom, with its centre at York where the ridings meet. The city is still practically encircled by its medieval walls. The minster dominates the city, with its three square towers, the largest church in the country and one of the largest in Christendom – suitably so for a Primate, Metropolitan of the Northern Province.

The splendour of this huge building has been brought out by the restoration and cleaning. It has survived many dangers, including the occasion when the lunatic brother of John Martin, the painter, set fire to it and destroyed all the medieval woodwork and the roofs. Earlier, the wonderful stained glass that survives in the cathedral and the score of city churches was saved by the public spirit of the Parliamentarian general Fairfax, who was also a patriotic Yorkshireman.

·Around the Close are lovely buildings from the past: the elaborately gabled treasurer's house, with its fascinating objects; St William's College with its seventeenth-century court; the ruins of St Mary's Abbey, once almost a rival to the minster in size. The abbot's house was taken over for the lord president's lodging – the King's Manor; it was enlarged by the swarthy Yorkshireman whose memory haunts it, the tragic Earl of Strafford. The Mansion House reminds us that York was the only city to rival London with a *lord* mayor. I remember the medieval Guildhall with its arcade of wooden columns of stout black oak, from the Forest of Galtres to the north of the city. This was gutted by bombs during the last war, but is now rebuilt. Ancient streets, like The Shambles and Stonegate, have survived with delightful, small, personal shops. Here and there remain buildings – halls of ancient craft guilds, alms-houses, decent Georgian houses with their proper proportions – testifying to a society in which people of taste had the lead. As an example, we have the columned Assembly Rooms, designed by Lord Burlington, strictly the most exquisite interior in York.

The city has been often painted, and it has been depicted in literature by the slightly epicene figure of Laurence Sterne, author of *Tristram Shandy* and *A Sentimental Journey*. His great-grandfather was archbishop, his uncle precentor, but his own domain is fixed at Shandy Hall, out at Coxwold, one of the most attractive villages in the noble North Riding. 'I sit down alone to venison, fish, and wild-fowl, or a couple of fowls or ducks, with curds, and strawberries and cream, and all the simple plenty which a rich valley can produce. I have a hundred hens and chickens about my yard – and not a parishioner catches a hare, or a rabbit, or a trout, but he brings it as an offering to me.' Such was Yorkshire fare and Yorkshire honesty in the summer of 1767.

At the other end of the village stands Newburgh Priory of the Fauconbergs, descendants of Oliver Cromwell, who used to preserve his skull there – as the old Catholic Easton family treasure the walking-staff of Sir Thomas More, their ancestor, at East Hendred in Berkshire. Many relics of the Puritan Protector are still about: a pillow-case and gloves are kept at Alnwick Castle in Northumberland; his christening robes came down in the family of the Frankland-Astley-Russells of Chequers. More moving were the bloodstained shirt and underclothes of the martyred Charles I, which were cherished by the family of his personal attendant, John Ashburnham (with whom he escaped from beleaguered Oxford – to be sold by the Scots). These relics had been 'touched' as late as last century, as a remedy for the King's Evil – such is human credulity.

DURHAM was the capital of a palatine bishopric – something comparable to the prince-bishoprics of Germany, Münster or Würzburg. This is at once clear from the overwhelming impression the cathedral and castle make on their rock above the Wear – 'Half church of

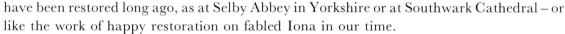

Right The Rows and old half-timbered houses combine to give Chester, in Cheshire, its historic and picturesque character.

Below The fortress town of Berwick-on-Tweed, on the Scottish frontier, was the residence of the Wardens of the East Marches.

have been restored long ago, as at Selby Abbey in Yorkshire or at Southwark Cathedral – or like the work of happy restoration on fabled Iona in our time.

Chester is the last of our frontier-towns, operative as such from Roman times to keep a watch on the wild tribesmen of North Wales. Thus Chester has had a fascinating and stormy history. It was not a normal county – nor was neighbouring Lancashire, which had complex historical origins; the Normans made Chester and its territory another palatinate, with its own jurisdiction, but a secular one. At the Reformation the monastic church was turned into a cathedral, and given Cheshire and much of Lancashire for its difficult diocese.

In the Civil War the city was hotly disputed between King and Parliament. In one of its sieges, the most original composer of the time, William Lawes (brother of Milton's friend, Henry), was killed – a wicked waste of an irreplaceable life – and he was mourned by the cultivated, art-loving King. The latter's turn was shortly to come: one has an image of his sad figure, looking out from the Phoenix Tower on the walls upon the rout of his last troops at Rowton Heath.

Chester deserves a high mark among English towns for having preserved so much of its historic legacy. Where other cities have disgraced themselves – notably Manchester and Nottingham – not only by failing to take the opportunities opened up by bombing during the last war but by the ill-advised rebuilding at their heart, Chester has been judicious. Practically all the medieval walls have survived and make a fascinating walk, from which one can enjoy many good sights. The Rows remain, with their arcades and old shops within; they are still more or less as Camden described them: 'The houses are very fair built, and along the chief streets are galleries or walking places they call Rows, having shops on both sides, through which a man may walk dry from one end to the other.'

Chester had an outlook not only upon north Wales, but towards Ireland. Until recent times it was a chief base for traffic across the Irish Channel. Mementoes of this are in some of the monuments in the cathedral to officials high up in the administration of Ireland, as also in the correspondence of Swift, often kept waiting for a crossing here by the weather, while his restless mind scribbled.

59

NORWICH is a true provincial capital, and the best we could possibly cite as such – as East Anglia is a true province with a character of its own. As Pevsner appreciates, 'Norwich has everything – a cathedral, a major castle on a mound right in the middle, walls and towers, an undisturbed medieval centre with winding streets and alleys, and a river with steamships, motor-yachts and sailing-boats.' Norwich had marked commercial prosperity in the later Middle Ages, which is visible in the magnificent array of medieval churches, greater than in any other city in the kingdom.

The cathedral is one of the most interesting in the country, with its soaring spire, its long nave and the inspiring way the choir lifts the eye (and heart) up at the east end. We owe it in essence again to the Normans. The Lady Chapel has a collection of medieval paintings of the Norwich School, rescued from the destruction of Reformation and Puritan fanatics. This reminds us that, of the artistic legacy of Britain, painting and sculpture suffered the worst losses. How terrible these were one appreciates from the superb mutilated figures – as fine as anything at Chartres – in the south-eastern transept at Lincoln, or from another masterly specimen at Winchester. At Norwich there is the memory of good Bishop Hall, early in the Civil War, locked in his palace while he could hear the miscreants hammering away in the cathedral.

The superb Norman keep of the castle remains, almost as large as and more decorative than the Tower of London. Within it is a museum of paintings of the East Anglian School – Constable, Gainsborough, Cotman, Crome – the province's chief contribution to the glory of the nation. East Anglian skies are peculiarly spacious, and these artists, especially Constable, give us unforgettable renderings of them, in all their freshness and variousness, which now light up the walls of galleries all over the world from California to Australia. Cotman, exquisite artist, sketched and painted hundreds of the buildings of his native province; he also etched and published them in book form. Norfolk has been better served in this way than any other county, and deservedly so – a tribute to the artistic patronage of connoisseurs in a previous age.

Right The Cathedral in Norwich (here seen from the Close) has perhaps the finest Norman nave in Britain. The stone spire soars above ancient Tombland which surrounds the Cathedral.

Left The fourteenth- and fifteenth-century cloisters of Norwich Cathedral are the largest in England.

The church of St Peter Mancroft in Norwich is situated next to the large and gaily-coloured market place.

Again the city has retained most of its walls, so too the Cathedral Close, with its fine medieval gateways, Sir Thomas Erpingham's (who comes into Shakespeare), St Ethelbert's and Bishop's Gate. The medieval churches offer a subject in themselves – one of the surplus ones has been turned into an admirable museum of church antiquities and treasures, as at York. The city possesses two of the finest of Dissenting chapels: the Old Meeting (Congregational) with a beautifully proportioned façade of 1693, and the more elaborate Octagon Chapel (Unitarian) of the mid-eighteenth century, with complete furnishings of the period within. This last was designed and built by one of the Norwich dynasty of Ivorys, who moved in the eighteenth century from trading in timber to joinery, thence to sculpture and architecture. An immense amount of good work in Norfolk houses was accomplished by this Georgian family. Matthew Brettingham was also a Norwich resident – one recalls his noble front at Kedleston – and hence he was chosen by the Duke of Norfolk to design Norfolk House in St James's Square (demolished in the 1930s). It would seem that an aesthete among guardian angels watched over Norwich.

Even in the 1930s the city authorities commissioned the finest City Hall of the period, upped on its mount between St Peter Mancroft and the medieval Guildhall, looking out over the lively spacious market-place. The latter is of flint set off by white stone dressings.

Among the agreeable associations of Norwich are some literary ones. The Tudor laureate John Skelton was an East Anglian. His 'Lament for Philip Sparrow' is about a favourite bird of one of the Black Nuns of Carrow, in the suburbs of Norwich. When she was asleep the little bird would make

> *Me often for to wake,*
> *And for to take him in*
> *Upon my naked skin.*
> *God wot, we thought no sin:*
> *What though he crept so low?*
> *It was no hurt, I trow,*
> *He did nothing, perdie,*
> *But sit upon my knee!*

Sir Thomas Browne, of *Religio Medici*, spent most of his life as a physician in the city, and wrote his distinctive books there. In the Victorian Age one associates Norwich with the eccentric figure of George Borrow, who went for a time to the Grammar School and then was apprenticed solicitor: one sees that overgrown boy who never grew up, lumbering about the streets and out across the heaths where were the gipsies of *Lavengro* and *The Romany Rye*.

3 CITY AND COUNTRY LANDMARKS

'WHAT LANCASHIRE THINKS TODAY England will think tomorrow' – such was the proud boast of Victorian Lancashire. As a result of the Industrial Revolution the secular balance of south against north was reversed in the nineteenth century. With the immense growth of the Lancashire cotton industry, Yorkshire woollens and steel, coal and iron in both, let alone coal and ship-building on Tyneside, the north outweighed the south for the first time in history and continued to do so up to 1914. This was made evident by the north's victory on Free Trade, carried through by Sir Robert Peel – of which we have visible evidence in the Free Trade Hall at Manchester. The two formative leaders in politics, Peel and Gladstone, were Lancashire men: the Peel fortune came from calico-printing; Gladstone's from importing cotton and sugar, and from the slave-trade. The chief landed magnates of Lancashire, the Derby family, wielded powerful influence in the Tory Party and produced a prime minister. Yorkshire fielded one in Herbert Henry Asquith, and produced a symptomatic Radical in John Morley; the Foreign Office was for long occupied by a northerner, though an aristocrat, in Sir Edward Grey.

OF THOSE LARGE northern cities the finest is Liverpool, though it has a runner-up in granite Newcastle upon Tyne. Liverpool has a grand situation on the wide Mersey; its character is dominantly Georgian, with a splendid collection of buildings in that style. One could observe a common theme in the axis running from London to Liverpool and on to Dublin – most observable now in Dublin where there has been less destruction. The grandest late Georgian monument in the country is St George's Hall, the work of Harvey Lonsdale Elmes, and the finest of its kind in all Europe – one knows nothing anywhere to equal it: it is very Greek in character, Liverpool's Parthenon. It dominates the area all round it: the neighbouring public buildings are in keeping, the Walker Art Gallery with its distinguished collection of paintings, and the columned Picton Reading Room.

The Town Hall itself is an excellent piece of earlier Georgian, in essence George II; the beautiful Bluecoat School is of the Queen Anne period. The classical inflexion continues in a number of streets and terraces: Rodney Street, where Gladstone was born, Hope Street and Gambier Terrace; though Abercromby Square has been spoiled by the university. Liverpool's heyday was the nineteenth century, when a local figure like William Roscoe could make a European reputation. A not very successful business man, his father a publican (a good Liverpool note), improbably a Unitarian, he made himself an authority on the Renaissance, and his books on it went into French, German and Italian.

The twentieth century has made dominating additions to this grand city: the florid and rhetorical buildings along Pierhead, the historic docks and the proud Mersey Tunnel. Most striking are the two new cathedrals punctuating the sky-line. Scott's Anglican cathedral has a romantic situation with the quarry of St James's cemetery behind; the central tower stands out nobly above the cliff-like masses of masonry from wherever one sees it. As a unified, integrated composition it is entirely successful, its colouring – pinkish sandstone – exquisite: the last such great church that will ever be built in this England.

Sir Edwin Lutyens' Roman Catholic cathedral was to have been even grander – and he was more original; but a church to rival St Peter's was a megalomaniac idea for a declining country (though he accomplished a splendid palace in the Viceroy's House in New Delhi): only the crypt at Liverpool was finished, and upon the platform above it a new cathedral succeeded in getting built after the war. This church, in challenging twentieth-century idiom, smaller and more original, is by Gibberd, to whom we also owe the finest re-housing development in London, in the East End at Poplar. Its tall lantern, a corona – the dedication is to Christ the King – makes its signal along the spine of the city to Sir Giles Scott's huge masculine tower.

Previous pages The fine waterfront at Liverpool on the River Mersey. The city of Liverpool, nucleus of the metropolitan county of Merseyside, forms an irregular crescent upon the north bank of the Mersey estuary, a few miles from the Irish Sea.

Gibberd's Roman Catholic Cathedral in Liverpool is built of concrete, glass and aluminium. Its central altar is surrounded by a cone-shaped building representing the Crown of Thorns.

MANCHESTER was the capital of Victorian Lancashire, a place of great distinction in its heyday. One sees that at its best in the novels of Mrs Gaskell – one of them with the symbolic title, *North and South* – whose husband was Unitarian minister of the Cross Street Chapel. Another expression was the *Manchester Guardian*, leading Liberal newspaper with a group of good writers around it and a more attentive following abroad than any English newspaper, except *The Times*. Actually, the Conservative newspaper from Leeds, *The Yorkshire Post* – which had a good anti-Appeasement record – though less literary, had a more responsible outlook. Manchester was the stamping ground of the Rochdale-born Radical orator, John Bright: Nonconformity incarnate.

Where Liverpool is classical, Manchester is Victorian Gothic. This is clearly visible in Alfred Waterhouse's vast Town Hall, filled with works of Victorian arts and crafts. Waterhouse was born in Liverpool, where his angular university building has more character than the nondescript works that have succeeded it. At Manchester the civic authorities have sadly failed to take the opportunities the heavy wartime bombing opened up for improving their city.

A few good buildings remain: certainly the John Rylands Library, with its superb collections of books and manuscripts. The Spencer Library from Althorp forms its nucleus, bought at one swoop by the widow of a textile manufacturer: this is what Manchester could do in its best days. The Whitworth Art Gallery has a good collection of pictures, especially of the Pre-Raphaelites, who were to the fore in Victorian times. The cathedral is just a large parish church; next door, Chetham's Hospital and Library speak up for the Middle Ages. In the neighbourhood only one country house is up to national standards – Heaton Park.

Here and there are good factory buildings of an earlier age. (It must be mentioned here that all these industrial cities have a far clearer atmosphere today than in the last century.)

Manchester Town Hall, a fine piece of Victorian architecture designed by Alfred Waterhouse, who also designed the University building.

Another example of Victorian architecture: the Town Hall at Leeds.

The Duke of Bridgewater's canal, begun in 1759 and constantly extended, made Manchester into a port, third in the country. Then came George Stephenson's triumphing railways, and Manchester became a metropolis.

OVER THE PENNINES, Yorkshire was hardly less important industrially than Lancashire. The rivalry goes back a long way, and was represented in the popular mind by the Lancashire–Yorkshire cricket-matches. Leeds is the capital of industrial Yorkshire, and deserves credit for its effort to achieve a civic centricity. It owes its many-columned Town Hall to the early Victorian Age; its Civic Hall, good in its siting and general impression, to ours.

Leeds has one church of national interest: St John's Briggate, a rare Caroline church complete with its Laudian woodwork, screens and all, which were given by John Harrison, cloth-merchant and benefactor, who rests there. When wandering through that rich and decorous interior one appreciates what the martyred Archbishop Laud stood for.

In the suburbs at Adel is a perfect little Norman church, of which Leeds people are very proud. They have even more reason to be proud of Temple Newsam, the grand Jacobean house which has made the most beautiful museum and art gallery of any I know. Not far out, too, is lovely Kirkstall Abbey, often painted, which comes very high in the class of ruins – along with Fountains and Tintern. Not far away from the city is Haworth, of such nostalgic memories; though the Brontës were not of Yorkshire stock, they speak for Yorkshire in literature, *Shirley* the representative novel of Victorian industry. In our time Phyllis Bentley has faithfully depicted Halifax; Priestley bats for Bradford (birthplace of Delius); while Herbert Read wrote a moving Yorkshire autobiography, *Annals of Innocence and Experience*.

The Tyne Bridge at Newcastle-upon-Tyne, built in 1928.

IT USED TO BE thrilling visually to go over one of the railway bridges that cross the Tyne, and look along that deep, sooty chasm, with all the rich colours of sunset, into Newcastle. One arrived at the station, with noble portico, the work of a fine architect of railway stations, John Dobson. He also designed that at Monkwearmouth; the railway station at Huddersfield (by Pritchett) is the best building in that town. Dobson built a good deal in and out of Newcastle, which did possess two handsome streets, Grey Street and Grainger Street; only some stretches of the former remain to show how superb the Victorian centre of the town was.

The cathedral is again a large parish church, notable for those monuments sculpted by John Flaxman and by John Bacon; there is an eloquent one to Cuthbert Collingwood, Nelson's second-in-command. The distinctive crown-and-spire nods to its companion over the Border, St Giles's in Edinburgh. More beautiful is the baroque church of All Saints, a rare oval, with elegant Wren-like tower in a commanding situation: it reminds me of the baroque churches of Dresden above its river.

Newcastle has kept most of its city walls, though the railway bashed unceremoniously into the castle and cut it up into pieces; chiefly the keep remains. The railways, with their bridges, dominate the Tyne, particularly George Stephenson's High-Level Bridge; appropriately, for the north east – based upon Darlington, where is the Railway Museum – was all Stephenson country.

Out beyond Newcastle, on the coast, is the most fabulous of Vanbrugh's creations, dramatic Seaton Delaval, more strictly beautiful than Blenheim, dominated by its central feature and with wings running deep to the centre, instead of laterally, and all the more romantic because the centre was gutted by fire. This marvellous house – on that exposed, bleak, coal-mining coast – has been largely rehabilitated in our time: a work of public spirit no less than of taste.

OF ANCIENT CITIES let us choose two: Lincoln in the east, Salisbury in the south, both indispensable monuments in the country's heritage. I think of Lincoln as an English Chartres, with those three towers rising and falling as one drives up along the Cliffe escarpment – just as the spires of Chartres appear and disappear with the ups and downs of the Beauce. Medievally, Lincoln had spires on top of those tall towers; the effect must have been stunning, the audacity of the builders tremendous. The cathedral is in every way spectacular, especially the west front as glimpsed coming in at the big Exchequer Gate. A large amount of Norman sculpture survives above the portals, the whole making a huge stone screen, English-fashion, as at Wells, Salisbury, or Exeter. Within, the Angel Choir is famous, the sculpture of the spandrels and of the bosses the finest in England: the former provides the smiling happy angels, the bosses luxuriate in flowers of the field – the English like to think that the love of nature is characteristic of them.

Lincoln is really two cities: cathedral and castle on the Roman site on top of the hill – hardly less spectacular than Durham – and, at the foot, the operative town of commerce, shops, trades, industry, but still containing a number of old churches. These two communities are connected directly by Steep Hill, a tremendous pull up for walkers and difficult enough to negotiate going down. All the way alongside are fascinating old buildings, two of which – known as Jews' houses from famous medieval Aaron – go right back to the twelfth century, along with another such at Exeter, the oldest in the country. All round the Close lie delectable residences, Georgian or earlier, ecclesiastical or legal, calling out for a Trollope to write up their domestic stories – as indeed he did, merging Exeter with Salisbury into Barchester.

On the opposite side to the ecclesiastical is the castle with its extensive bailey, now walkable grounds. The castle formed, as was frequently the case till recent times, the Gaol; from it De Valera escaped after the Easter Rising in Dublin. Today one can inspect the Gaol

71

chapel: a rarity with its cubicles so arranged that the prisoners could not communicate with each other.

On the green lower slopes below the Close is the Usher Art Gallery, well filled with water-colours of the Lincolnshire scene, Peter de Wint and David Cox. It has too a good collection of manuscripts of Tennyson, who was born at Somersby across the wolds and spoke with a strong Lincolnshire burr. Up on the hill is one of those cosy historic hostelries which visitors, especially Americans (see Henry James), associate with the idea of England: the White Hart. How right they are, and how comfortable one has been made, with what good cheer, in any number of these establishments! Solid, decent old furniture, good pieces of china, gay chintzes and cushions in deep chairs, country food, drink according to taste, early morning tea brought to one in bed – what bliss I have encountered over the years in traditional English inns! Certainly they are an endearing part of the heritage: such places as the George at Glastonbury, the Swan at Wells, the Angel at Grantham, the Hop Pole at Tewkesbury; at Exeter the old Clarence, and the Imperial with its garden; at Stratford, the Swan's Nest, the Shakespeare or the Falcon, or out at Welcombe, the country house with its garden, where the historian G. M. Trevelyan was born. More remote is the Peacock at Rowsley in Derbyshire, or the inn at Helmsley in the Vale of Pickering, below the wonderful terraces that look down on Rievaulx. At Devizes there is still the inn whose host's little boy used to make a few shillings by drawing the guests: he made a fortune later as Sir Thomas Lawrence.

And some there are that have no name. But what memories they have for one, what places, country houses, castles, cathedrals, churches, towns, they have enabled one to see! Some are gone: the Red Lion at Truro, 1671 above its door, a grand oak staircase up to a long Queen Anne parlour from which one watched the bustle of Boscawen Street below. Or there was the famous George at Salisbury. . . . Of all these places of refreshment and merriment the poet was, of course, Dickens.

Right Lincoln Cathedral, of Norman and Gothic construction, overlooks the city. Formerly each tower was topped by a spire, even more impressive.

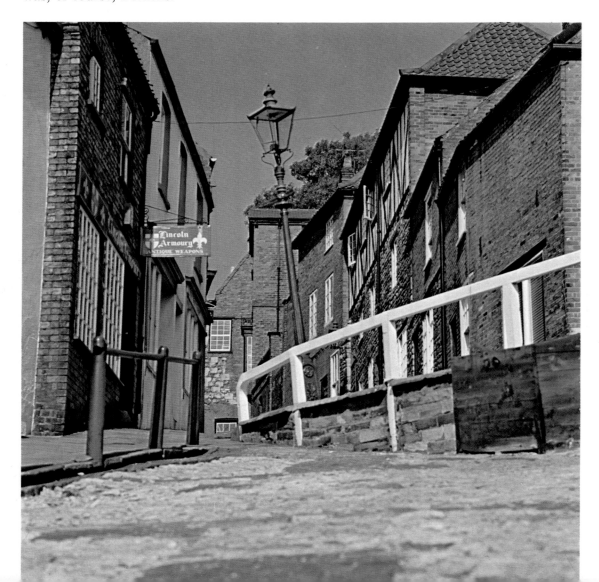

The cathedral city of Lincoln, which was a significant Roman town, known as Lindum Colonia, from which the name derives.

Salisbury Cathedral, which has the highest spire in England.

SALISBURY TOO began on a hill: the sensational Iron Age encampment of Old Sarum, within which the Normans built castle and cathedral, but where there was little water. In the twelfth century the city descended into the meadows where there was plenty; in the next century they erected the new cathedral, and in the next that work of genius, the tapering spire which is beyond compare in the English-speaking world. One sees it at the end of every road approaching the city, and across the water-meadows that surround it on every side.

Salisbury cathedral is the most unified and perfect of English cathedrals, rising out of the sea of green lawns all round it; and beyond that the most satisfying collection of houses – Bishop's Palace, Deanery, canonries, almonries, chapelries, song-school – of all periods and of diversified interest and beauty of anywhere in England. No wonder Constable was fascinated by the scene, especially by the shapely shrine itself, and painted it in all moods under the Wiltshire skies. One sees the results as far away as the Huntington Art Gallery in California. The Close, too, has its own perfection, natural, spontaneous, unplanned: merely the result of good taste, as it prevailed in previous centuries.

Nor is the city unsatisfying, its streets still following the medieval lay-out, beyond the walled Close. It has its own parish churches of interest, many decent houses still, a stately Guildhall and Georgian Council House. The trouble here is that the central area is swamped by traffic, since Salisbury is a busy shopping town as well as much visited by tourists.

For me, the shades that haunt it are not of bishops, distinguished as some have been – especially the mathematician Seth Ward, friend of Wren, whose work may be seen in the design of the Matrons College the bishop founded, recovering things after the Civil War. My man is naughty Simon Forman, who went to school in the Close, practised medicine and astrology in Fisherton Street, and wrote that rarity, an Elizabethan autobiography. More recently, there is Edith Olivier, a daughter of the Church, who wrote her delightful books about city and county, Wilton and Wiltshire. Or I seem to see the figure of saintly George Herbert in King Charles's days, walking in from Bemerton to hear evensong in the loveliest of English cathedrals.

There are medieval canons' houses still standing in Salisbury Close, and others like Mompesson House, which was built in about 1670.

BATH is, of all English towns, the one that most nearly approaches perfection. This is because it was mostly planned and executed in the eighteenth century when the best aristocratic taste prevailed, and Bath was the spa *par excellence* of the aristocracy from London and the gentry from all over the country. The north had its spa at Buxton, where the Dukes of Devonshire built the fine Crescent. Harrogate rose with Yorkshire industry in the nineteenth century.

Bath was inspired by men touched with genius. Ralph Allen, the Cornishman who made a fortune by reorganizing the country's postal service, devoted it to good works. He was behind Bath's development, promoted the use of its beautiful stone not only in the city but elsewhere throughout the south – Beaumont Street at Oxford, for example, or Lemon Street at Truro. He backed the elder and younger Woods in their imaginative and elegant building schemes: squares, terraces, crescents, taking advantage of that dramatic hilly situation. He set an example with his Prior Park, grandest of Palladian villas, with its chapel still unchanged. Immensely philanthropic, he was a good friend to writers and artists. Pope wrote of him,

> *Let humble Allen, with an awkward shame,*
> *Do good by stealth and blush to find it fame.*

Fielding celebrated him in *Tom Jones* as Squire Allworthy.

The city reached the height of its fame in the days of Jane Austen, who put it into *Persuasion* – one sees her shade tripping down Milsom Street still. The buildings these people knew or were responsible for are still happily there. The Abbey is the most uniform of Perpendicular churches, with its complete fan-vaulting; this and the Perpendicular style are the two characteristic English contributions to architecture. One misses the glass and interior woodwork which it once possessed, but in place are the scores of monuments and tablets which one can read as a supplement to Jane Austen or Fielding or Smollett's novels.

The Assembly Rooms I rate along with those at York as the most distinguished I know; the Pump Room, Guildhall, Palladian Bridge in keeping. Then comes the magnificent sequence of squares and terraces, Queen Square, Circus, Royal Crescent, Lansdown Crescent, spanning those slopes. What reason we have to be grateful to that imaginative co-operation, to Ralph Allen and the Woods, and Beau Nash who led the social dance and enforced good manners. Bath reigned supreme until the rise of Brighton, with the Prince Regent's fantasy pleasure-dome of the Pavilion and his patronage that led to those colour-washed squares and terraces, no less elegant but gayer and more light-hearted, lit by the sparkle of the sea.

Both Bath and Brighton were projections of aristocratic London, Georgian and Regency. Each had its reflections in the surrounding countryside. One of the Woods built accomplished Faringdon House, home of Poet Laureate Pye. The office and succession of Poet Laureate is another English speciality. It has contained some great names, Dryden and Tennyson, along with distinguished ones from Southey to Bridges and Masefield, and on to Betjeman in our time, with an eye as sensitive for our architectural tradition as an ear for verse.

Just outside Bath, Claverton manor (a fine villa by Wyattville) adds a new feature to Britain's heritage: an American Museum illustrating American life from earliest colonial days. This is just as much a projection of the traditional heritage at home as the country houses of Virginia, the townships of New England or the Delaware, or the many colonial churches with portico and spire following Gibbs's model of St Martin-in-the-Fields.

Bath has had its reflections not only in literature and the arts – portrait-painters like Gainsborough had their Bath period when they painted visitors there for the season. A successful Cornish doctor, Dr Oliver, patented a kind of biscuit, Bath Olivers. Specialities of this sort go back much earlier – Banbury cakes and Chelsea buns.

We have seen that Bath goes back to Roman times – clients came from all over the western empire to its beneficent (and surprisingly hot) waters. In Anglo-Saxon times King Edgar

The city of Bristol seen from the Cabot Tower, built in commemoration of John Cabot. Bristol owed its wealth to trade, dealing mainly in exports of wool and cloth, and imports of wine.

was crowned here, and the nucleus of the coronation rite by which English monarchs have been crowned goes right back to the form used then. The baths were very fashionable and promiscuously resorted to in Elizabethan days – Shakespeare speaks in the Sonnets of resorting thither for cure of love's distemper. It was Beau Nash who imposed Augustan order upon the assemblies, as the Woods upon the buildings. A European judgment tells us that 'as a piece of town planning, Georgian Bath is unique in England and indeed in Europe'. This is remarkable in a people who rather pride themselves, mistakenly or no, upon their indisposition to planning in their affairs.

OF ALL ENGLISH provincial cities, Bristol was the most diversely interesting and historically rewarding – it had so much in it from all periods, especially the medieval. But it suffered horribly from bombing in the Second World War – after it, I remember standing on Bristol Bridge in tears to see the shells of half-a-dozen medieval churches gutted. Before the war they were full of monuments from which one could read much of the history of the city. I remember still that of the benefactor Edward Colston.

Today the chancel of the cathedral, formerly abbey, is thought especially significant in the development of architecture. St Mary Redcliffe has always been held the grandest of parish churches, a monument to the civic pride of medieval merchants. Queen Elizabeth thought it the 'fairest' on her visit, when prayers were offered up for her 'preservation on so dangerous a journey'. The charming Merchant Venturers' Almshouses of the seventeenth century remain, though damaged. This suggests – as Bristol does, more than any city except London – so many themes. The Merchant Venturers, in the later Middle Ages, were responsible for the expansion of trade into the Atlantic; from that flowed the pioneering voyages of the Cabots to the New World.

Originally a Roman town, then a place of note in Saxon times (King Edgar was crowned there in 973), Bath assumed the character we know today in the Georgian period, when the two architects John Wood, father and son, virtually re-designed it. A perfect example of their architectural style is the noble sweep of the Royal Crescent (*left*).

Right The Pulteney Bridge spans the River Avon at Bath, a classic example of the Palladian style of building.

Right Bath Abbey seen from the baths. The Abbey Church of St Peter and St Paul is a fine example of late Perpendicular architecture.

The city has any number of ancient almshouses, hospitals, schools, witnessing the merchant wealth and public spirit in former times. All over the country there are such foundations: at Abingdon the pretty buildings of four such are an ornament to that ancient town. Nottingham destroyed some of its almshouses; Guildford has kept the foundation of Archbishop Abbot, with its noble gatehouse, at the top of the High Street – which has with some effort retained most of its historic look. All over England there are these relics of old kindness and charitableness. One passes them sometimes by the roadside as at Froxfield, driving into pleasant Marlborough with its excellent Public School (the main old building an outsize Queen Ann coaching inn).

Bristol has a unique monument in its Theatre Royal, with unspoiled interior, from the mid-eighteenth century, the oldest playhouse still in use. I recall a similar early theatre at the other end of the country in the market-square at Richmond in Yorkshire. Bristol has many Georgian buildings – the finest, the Exchange, by the elder Wood. It too has its squares – the grandest, Queen Square, civically damaged even before being bombed – and terraces reaching up to Clifton, which had a spell as a spa. Here the Suspension Bridge, 'the most beautiful of English suspension bridges', by that romantic engineer, Brunel, bespeaks the creative spirit of the Industrial Revolution. This spirit is clearly visible in its bridges: one sees it again in the Menai Suspension Bridge, or the elegance of Brunel's Tamar Bridge with curved approaches and double span.

Gratefully, some of the Georgian buildings of Bristol have been saved by being made use of by the university. But it has also made its twentieth-century contribution with the huge Wills Tower, which has already become one of the focal points of the city – and in so short a time. It was a curious, and audacious, form for a university building to take: a Gothic monument, in this age, with demonstrative ceremonial staircase and entrance hall.

This area, with Somerset at the heart, has the finest church towers in England: the Somerset type, of tall design, decorative top stage and gathered pinnacles pointing to heaven, which can be seen as far east as Magdalen tower at Oxford, as far west as Probus in Cornwall. Passing through Taunton in the train one looks out for the three familiar towers which signalize that town. Appropriately, Lincolnshire offers the best church spires – such noble designs and heights as one sees at Louth and Grantham aloft above the wolds, and many hardly less grand piercing the wider skies over the flat lands. Tallest tower of all is that of Boston, the Boston Stump, signalling its message from the ages of faith out over fenland and sea.

CHURCH TOWERS OF BRITAIN:
Above left Magdalen Tower, Oxford, with its decorative top stage and gathered pinnacles, and two Lincolnshire towers: (*above*) The fine church tower and spire at Louth, and (*right*) the tallest church tower in Britain, ironically called Boston Stump.

The architecture of a house generally reflects the building materials available in that particular area. For example (*left*) the Clifton Maybank Porch on the west front of Montacute House in Somerset, is built of 'snuff-coloured' Ham Hill stone, while (*right*) Little Moreton Hall in Cheshire is a fine example of the black-and-white timbering peculiar to a part of England where no building-stone is readily available.

A PRIME ADVANTAGE of an old country is that its visual experiences are so much more varied; for the architecture – buildings, whole towns and villages – expresses the geology of the district, and thus the local character of the materials. There is immeasurable diversity. If one were blindfolded and set down in an historic town or village, one could very often tell where one was on having the blindfold removed. It really is rather extraordinary that a trained eye should be able at once to tell whether the building is fourteenth- or fifteenth-century, or whether the first half or the second, or, more remarkably, often within a decade. Scooting along the road one can tell at a glance whether the gate-piers to house or church are seventeenth-century, or nineteenth-century pretending to be seventeenth or twentieth wishing to look like eighteenth.

Splendid building-stones are available in most parts of the island, especially along the oolite ridge running from Somerset to Northamptonshire and Rutland. Thus the beautiful snuff-coloured Ham Hill stone of Somerset houses like Montacute and the Perpendicular churches and towers; or the golden stone tinged with brown of Northamptonshire in such places as Higham Ferrers or Oundle; or the cream of Ketton, the white mottled with blue of Clipsham. There are the red sandstones of Devon and the north-west, hence of Exeter, Chester, Carlisle, of so beautiful a church as Lanercost Priory, or Naworth Castle of the Howards. Dorset has a silvery chalk stone; Yorkshire millstone grit; Aberdeen its austere grey granite, Cornwall a greener granite speckled with quartz.

Where there is no building-stone we have the flint of East Anglia and Kent; the black-and-white timbering of the Severn Valley all up to Cheshire and Lancashire (see many halls like Moreton Old Hall or Samlesbury). In eastern counties we have plaster and pargetting, and everywhere brick to supply the want of stone, brick of various colours and shapes as in London, the Home Counties, Cambridge colleges.

Where there is such an embarrassment of riches one can only select, and one's choice can only be personal.

If we consider sea-coast towns first, the most sensational is Brighton. Like Bath much of the original core was planned, and thus the Regency squares and terraces show up nobly. It went on developing into the Victorian Age, of which it is as much a monument; the secular building continued the classical idiom on the whole, the churches Gothic – two of them masterpieces, neither ever finished, J. L. Pearson's All Saints and St Bartholomew, its tremendous height making an unforgettable impact. The glory of Brighton – and the clue to the whole place – is the Prince Regent's Pavilion, a work of pure fantasy and beauty, Indian in its external style, with domes and minarets, Chinese in its interior. Its fantastic character is true to its creator, for the Regent was a *fantaisiste*, reality in all its ugliness was too much for him. It was for long derided: Sydney Smith said that it looked as if the dome of St Paul's had gone down to the seaside and pupped; but, though he was a wit, there is no evidence that he was a man of taste.

Moreover, the Pavilion in its overwhelming orientalism has a significant historical reference. Those were days in which British rule in India was growing into an empire. The great pro-consul, Warren Hastings, and the scholar of genius, Sir William Jones, had an absorbing interest in Indian culture and literature. Something of this was reflected in the paintings of William Daniell and William Hodges, as in the portraits of Tilly Kettle. The Pavilion remains as witness to those historic relations – as does also beautiful Sezincote near Anglo-Indian Cheltenham. In literature too: President Rhadakrishnan told me that, after all has been said, Kipling's *Kim* is the book that best understands and penetrates to the essential India.

A world away from Brighton is Whitby, with its extraordinarily strong personality: that

Cheltenham, in Gloucestershire, is a spa town on the edge of the Cotswolds: The three mineral springs were discovered there in 1716 and the town rapidly became popular after a visit by George III in 1788. Much of the gracious Georgian town plan remains, including the Imperial Gardens, pictured here.

The future King George IV, then Prince of Wales, brought his patronage to Brighton in 1783. The Royal Pavilion was his inspiration. This fantasy palace now houses a museum and art gallery.

chasm in the exposed coastal plateau letting in a long inlet of the North Sea. This made Whitby's importance and fortune. High upon the cliff, soaring to heaven, stand the ruins of St Hilda's Abbey: the central tower was standing as late as the eighteenth century, the Early English west front damaged by German bombardment in the First World War. Down below is the ancient town, a huddle of red-tiled roofs, the inlet crowded with shipping.

That chasm reminds one of a comparable, much smaller breach in the cliffs in Cornwall, the twisting snake-like inlet at Boscastle, jade-green rocks and water – that place so beloved by Thomas Hardy. He met his wife at the church above, St Juliot, and wrote some of his finest poems about the coast and places there:

O the opal and the sapphire of that wandering western sea . . .

Two of the seaports in Cornwall remain characteristic and unspoiled: Fowey and Padstow, one on the exposed Atlantic north coast, the other on the quieter Channel coast, looking across to Brittany. Each has a precipitous descent down to the quays by its river, narrow streets with gabled houses, openings giving a glimpse of water, source of the little towns' livelihood through the centuries. Each is dominated by an historic house, called

On the cliff above the picturesque port of Whitby in Yorkshire stands the ruin of St Hilda's Abbey, founded in 656. Whitby has been an important fishing town and whaling port, and was the home of Captain James Cook, whose voyages round the world (1769–75) were made in wooden ships built at Whitby.

86

The fourteenth-century church and huddled roofs of Fowey on the south coast of Cornwall dominate the west bank of the sheltered Fowey estuary.

Place, for it was the barton, or 'place', of a neighbouring monastery: Place at Padstow, built about the time of the Armada, looking south over deer-park and the wide expanse of the Camel estuary (sung in Betjeman's poems); and the other Place at Fowey – medieval, Henry VIII, and Regency Gothic – dominating from its bulwarks the town's humped roofs and keeping an eye on harbour-mouth for what might come in from the open sea. Each is still lived in by its proper family, Prideaux and Treffrys.

Go up the Irish Channel to look at Conway: a town, four-square within its walls, of that king, Edward I, who hammered the Welsh and built all those castles, Caernarvon, Pembroke, Harlech, to pen them in. Conway castle may serve to instance them, still fairly complete though roofless: an example of the latest, up-to-date castle-building after the model of Savoy of the late thirteenth century. Conway also has the finest Elizabethan town-house in Wales, Plas Mawr, running back longways from the street. Next door is the crescent-shaped, northward-looking – like Santander – Victorian resort of Llandudno, beautifully placed between Great and Little Orme. The whole complex of town, estuary, castle, bridges, crescent sands, mountains in the background, the island of Anglesey – fabled Mona, haunt of the Druids – is of a hardly realized European significance.

Let us go right across the Midlands to King's Lynn, at the angle of the Wash, of fascinating interest: a town of red-brick Georgian houses, two spreading market-places – Saturday Market and Tuesday Market, with their old inns. Each area has its medieval church: St Margaret's with grand two-tower façade and the finest brasses within; St Nicholas' Chapel with pretty Victorian spire and magnificent lectern, like that which the monks of Byron's Newstead abbey threw in disgust into their pond at the Reformation, subsequently fished up to ornament Southwell cathedral. King's Lynn (formerly Bishop's Lynn) has a medieval Guildhall, of flint and stone chequer-pattern, eighteenth-century Assembly Rooms and an exquisite Wren-type Customs House, like that at Poole. Or like the beautiful Town Hall at Abingdon, standing on its own looking across to medieval abbey gatehouse and Elizabethan grammar-school.

Rounding the western end of the Wash – all this alluvial land the richest soil agriculturally – we come to two towns of distinguished appearance a little inland, but living by the sea: in this like so much of England, nowhere is one far from the sea. Both Spalding and Wisbech have something about them of Holland, to which they have long been allied by trade and horticulture. Spalding is famous for tulips, but also for its inheritance from the eighteenth century: Georgian houses facing each other across tree-lined banks of the River Welland, distinguished buildings expressive of the cultivated spirit which formed a Gentlemen's Society of Antiquaries (twentieth-century Spalding has done some things to deface itself).

We may take this society as a prototype of the many such gatherings of cultivated people all over the country, which improved on its beauty, promoted landscaping, the planting of parks, the building of country houses, exploring antiquities, forwarding the publication of local histories. Practically every English county, in the eighteenth century, exemplified such enterprise. The results remain in the magnificent series of county histories: Hasted's *Kent*, Surtees' *Durham*, Lipscomb's *Buckinghamshire*, Hutchins' *Dorset*, Baker's *Northamptonshire*, Ormerod's *Cheshire*, and so many more – all with their engraved plates of the houses they built; often with the regular grouping of squire's mansion, church and rectory, the landscape

The medieval Trinity Guildhall at King's Lynn, Norfolk, with its Renaissance porch, is beautifully decorated in flint and stone chequer-pattern.

groomed around them, of which they were so proud, and had reason to be, for never was it more beautiful.

STRATFORD-UPON-AVON lies at the heart of England, in more senses than one. It was already celebrated in the very next generation after Shakespeare's, witness Sir William Dugdale, in that 'it gave birth and sepulture to our late famous poet'. The whole town speaks of him; if he were to come back to it, after some three and a half centuries, he would find it still recognizable. All things considered, it is surprising that it has kept so much and changed so little: the overwhelming memory has acted as a preservative.

One can watch the progress of his life in the buildings that remain. Up in Henley Street is the sixteenth-century home of his father's family, the interior not so much changed: living-room downstairs, upstairs the big bedroom of good middle-class folk – his father, the glover, very active in the town's affairs, his mother, Mary Arden, from out at Wilmcote (where the house remains) something more. For the Ardens were gentlefolk, or near it. In the centre of the town the Grammar School survives – many such Elizabethan schools survive all over the country – with the Gild Chapel convenient next door.

Hugh Clopton's long fifteenth-century bridge is still there – the road that led to London and the success that enabled him to buy New Place, across the lane from school and chapel. This building is, alas, the one loss in the centuries since, when neighbouring houses survived. One Elizabethan inn, the White Swan, still has the panels of the story of Tobit painted in Shakespeare's lifetime. The big collegiate church is full of tombs and monuments, some of them of townsfolk he knew: his friend John Combe, for instance, who died a couple of years before him; or Richard Hill, grazier, who died when the poet was writing his poems and sonnets for his patron; or the grandee Earl of Totnes, who married the heiress of Clopton, still there up across the fields. Within the chancel his own family are gathered together, his figured bust looking out upon it all – as the tall spire, reflected in the waters of the Avon, beckons across the meadows to Clifford Chambers, where that other Warwickshire poet, Michael Drayton, spent his summers.

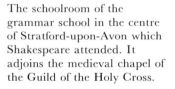

The schoolroom of the grammar school in the centre of Stratford-upon-Avon which Shakespeare attended. It adjoins the medieval chapel of the Guild of the Holy Cross.

Warwick is the county town, and is among the first of my choice as a representative English town. It is dominated by its castle, rising sheer from the sounding river below, which in Shakespeare's time was occupied by the Dudleys, much favoured by Elizabeth I, succeeded there by a fellow poet, Fulke Greville, whose family still remains. Within, the castle is full of treasures, especially pictures: no historic residence that I know more so.

The church is hardly less remarkable, for its upstanding eighteenth-century Gothick tower, visible all over the countryside; and for its monuments. The Beauchamp Chapel has the eloquent brass effigy of the fifteenth-century Earl of Warwick, with all its crests: Shakespeare's patron would find in the Sonnets

thy monument
When tyrants' crests and tombs of brass are spent.

Cheek by jowl are the Dudley tombs: Elizabeth I's favourite, Leicester, and the wife whom the Queen detested, with the little boy, the 'noble imp', who was their hope – his small suit of mail, as page to the Queen, is in the castle. Elsewhere, away from the Dudleys, is the huge tomb of Fulke Greville (slain by his servant in the castle), and an early example of pure classicism, in black and white marble, by Nicholas Stone, first of English sculptors in the revived art with the patronage of King Charles.

The town is no less packed with interest: Leicester's pretty hospital, with chapel over the West Gate; an East Gate with fanciful eighteenth-century Gothick chapel above. Admirable Georgian houses bespeak the human scale and sense of proportion of that age, out of which rise above the domestic scene both Shire Hall and Court House. Georgian Warwick produced a notable architect in Francis Smith, who designed country houses hereabouts. His masterpiece is the noble front of Stoneleigh Abbey, where Jane Austen visited her rich relations, the Leighs.

In spite of a great fire in 1694 a number of Tudor timbered houses survive in Warwick, like the Lord Leycester Hospital (or Maison Dieu) which dates from 1415.

The Beauchamp Chapel in St Mary's Church, Warwick, was built in 1443–64 as a memorial to Richard Beauchamp, Earl of Warwick, and it is his fine brass effigy which lies on a Purbeck marble tomb chest in the Chapel.

As these towns lean towards the west so Stamford, in Lincolnshire – my next choice – leans towards the east. It is indeed a fascinating town: half-a-dozen medieval churches, its streets full of good buildings of the sixteenth, seventeenth and eighteenth centuries – think of it! It lay on the Great North Road, hence its early importance for trade, and the welcoming hostelries like the Stamford and the George. Thank heaven, this jewel of a town is now by-passed and has a hope of preserving itself. The spire of All Saints Church on the rise dominates it, looking down the street to the bridge at the bottom, the entry from the south.

In St Mary's Church lies Sir David Phillips, Welsh follower of Henry VII to Bosworth,

which made his fortune for him and his young relation, David Cecil – hence the rise of that fortunate family. Its greatest member, Lord Burghley – Elizabeth's minister for forty years and architect of the success of the reign – lies in St Martin's in an alabaster six-poster, with the lord treasurer's staff in hand. (His clever son and successor, Robert, lies similarly at Hatfield on his tomb: a more sophisticated work of art by Maximilian Colt, whom he selected for his royal mistress's tomb in Westminster Abbey.) The senior branch of this historic family lives on here in the palace Lord Burghley built just outside the town. He collected sufficient estates in those forty years to build up a southern territory for the junior line around Theobalds – which decayed from the Civil War; luckily canny Robert had transferred himself to Hatfield before the deluge.

Several of the senior line are together in this church – as Lord Burghley's Hospital of 1597 still exists outside it. Great Elizabethans thought it proper to pay tribute in charity for their prosperity – like American millionaires today. This was, however, but carrying on the tradition from the Middle Ages: Browne's Hospital, almshouses and chapel, from the 1480s, also survive. Everywhere are goodly houses, and little 'places', of the finest building-stone from the country round – Ketton and Barnack, and Collyweston (to which Henry VII's pious mother, the Lady Margaret, retired) just over the hill.

Lewes in Sussex has not Stamford's medieval churches, but it has the most attractive long High Street, full of variety from the sixteenth to the nineteenth centuries: red brick, silvery brick and older timber-framed houses. The Reformation lost it its splendid Cluniac priory in the meadows below – blown up by gunpowder, on the orders of Thomas Cromwell.

Another hilly High Street comes to mind, Burford, gateway to the Cotswolds – that thrilling view down to the bridge over the lovely Windrush, past house after house of fascinating interest. For Burford has medieval houses, like Hill House with early hall within, arched doorway to enter. Farther down is the Great House, impressive as an example of a sophisticated town-house: a Queen Anne Italian *palazzo* extending its length backwards from its street-front. Farther down yet one glimpses with joy the coloured front of a baroque mansion, rich brick with stone dressings – now, improbably, a Nonconformist chapel, urns along the parapet removed as 'inconsistent with the sacred character of the building'.

The church, its spire an eye-catcher all down the Windrush valley, is packed with interest inside its complex fabric: the medieval woodwork, screens, glass, even paintings have survived the (needless) horrors of the Reformation. Among unnumbered monuments one chapel is filled with the vast structure of the Elizabethan Southwark School of carvers – Johnsons, Cures, Christmases – a memorial to the grandparents of Lord Falkland, who appears on it as a boy. He made these parts famous, attracting to his house at Great Tew (the terraces where they walked remain) the most sympathetic of the figures from Oxford in King Charles's time – the philosophic William Chillingworth, the poet Sidney Godolphin, Gilbert Sheldon and John Morley and John Hales, the young Thomas Hobbes and Edward Hyde, in those halcyon years before the Civil War. Hyde, as Earl of Clarendon, described it unforgettably in his exile abroad. When all is said, Falkland, killed at the battle of Newbury, has as worthy a place in our memory as John Hampden, whom one sees riding across Chalgrove Field, the other side of Oxford, his head drooping, mortally wounded, to die in an inn at Thame.

Of hill towns, those rarities in England, let us select Bridgnorth and Rye. Bridgnorth has a grand situation terraced above the Severn. Much of it was destroyed in the Civil War, and thus was rebuilt in the best period, from Restoration to Regency. The church is by a bridge-builder, Thomas Telford, and well-placed visually, as most of the public buildings are, closing or punctuating vistas properly – as infrequently in England. This town has style. Rye, on the other hand, has charm: a huddle of pleasant Georgian houses and red-tiled roofs, a grand Caroline school – Peacock's of 1636 – and Lamb House of that lumbering shade and endearing memory, Henry James, who loved the place.

WHERE CAN WE STOP, where there are so many from which to choose? As for villages, there are scores, if not hundreds, that have come down to us to convey the idea of England in all its variety – let alone Wales and Scotland. Let us diminish in size as we go, down to hamlets. Not a few of these little places have been sung by the poets. We can only stumble along regionally, even then inadequately – and invidiously.

Sherborne, for example, is not inferior to any of the smaller towns, with its snuff-coloured building-stone, pleasant houses, abbey church like a cathedral, historic school, a spreading, winged castle of Sir Walter Ralegh and the Digbys, besides the ruins of the medieval castle and a Caroline church standing at the gates to greet the connoisseur. Henley-on-Thames is in total contrast: two good Georgian streets of red brick, a bulky church and tower dominating the eighteenth-century bridge over the Thames, swans on the river, punts, barges, canoes, and all the ritual paraphernalia of rowing.

Chipping Camden in Gloucestershire ('Chipping' means 'market') was an important medieval wool town. The Perpendicular style 'wool' church of St James is of Cotswold stone.

The early seventeenth-century cottages of Arlington Row, Bibury, in the Cotswolds.

But these are towns. Dorchester in Oxfordshire is a village, with a tremendous abbey church of immense architectural significance, another eighteenth-century bridge, fascinating old coaching inns, especially the George at the corner opposite the church. Across the meadows is Wallingford with its Anglo-Saxon earthen ramparts – and *two* local heroes. Sir William Blackstone, the jurist, is in the church (his house by the bridge): his *Commentaries on the Laws of England* exerted more influence on English and American law than any other book, except possibly Coke's *Institutes*. A more beneficent shade is Agatha Christie, beloved by all the world, who now lies in Cholsey churchyard.

Not far away, Ewelme possesses rarities – a noble church with the tomb of Chaucer's grand-daughter, the Duchess of Suffolk, and her foundation: almshouses around a court-yard, at one corner a fifteenth-century school, at another country lodgings for the Regius Professor of Medicine at Oxford – much appreciated by Canadian Sir William Osler, with his sense of the past as acute as his genius as a physician.

The Cotswolds hold the prize for English villages. They have such an exquisite setting, hills and valleys with beechwoods, the finest building-stone of which the best architectural use has been made, roofs of grey Stonesfield slate with which the medieval colleges of Oxford are roofed. Thus we have inherited a score of beautiful villages from earlier centuries, many with good churches and some with splendid houses. Such are Chipping Camden, Bibury, Broadway beneath its towering hill, the western escarpment of the Cotswolds; Bourton-on-the-Hill, Bourton-on-the-Water, Lower Slaughter, the Barringtons, Swinbrook, and many others.

Suffolk comes next, with the splendours of its churches, their speciality of angel-roofs – the medieval world made little distinction between fantasy and reality, so heaven was very real to them in their roofs and wall-paintings, dooms and judgments. Long Melford is very grand for a village, with its half-dozen houses of the size of manor houses, besides the big Elizabethan house at the top. Lavenham is no less remarkable, with more houses of the medieval and Tudor clothiers – indeed Kersey gave its name to one of the varied types of cloth they made. This is flint country for the churches, with brick and timber-framed houses in the villages, their plaster surfaces often decorated by pargetting, a Suffolk speciality. One thinks of Clare with its colour-washed houses, or Stoke-by-Nayland with the tower that appears so nostalgically in Constable's pictures, or Flatford Mill again in that landscape much given to mill-houses and windmills with their sails – in old days bringing a touch of the sea inland.

East Anglia has been lucky in producing so many good painters, rivalled only by Devon with Nicholas Hilliard, Turner, Reynolds, not to forget James Northcote, Richard Cosway, Sir Charles Eastlake, or Luny among marine painters. Devon villages include Clovelly, unique with its precipitous steps all the way down the cliff to the quay, fishermen's cottages climbing up, with lobster-pots and fuchsias. I particularly love country on the edges of the

Left The Mill at Lower Slaughter in Gloucestershire.

Below The old Guildhall at Lavenham, Suffolk.

high moor, Dartmoor, or Exmoor or Bodmin Moor – such as Manaton in Devon, with solid yeomen's houses around the green.

The 'solid yeomen's houses' of Manaton, Dartmoor, Devon, around the village green in springtime.

In Cornwall there is Blisland. A proper village should have church and rectory, the squire's house hard by, a pub and shop or two, a post office and a green. Blisland has all these, a granite village looking sideways down the valley of the Camel, a salmon- and trout-stream. The church of St Protus and St Hyacinth has everything that a Cornish church should have: roodscreen and loft, angels, saints, holy-water stoup, vestments, bells – including sanctus-bell to let the parish know it is being prayed for. At the end of the green is the original mansion – recently restored with good feeling and public spirit; beside the church the early Victorian rectory; lower down the valley the rambling mansion of the Recusant Kemps, Lavethan, also recently put back into good shape. Lucky village! St Protus and St Hyacinth seem to look after it well.

Another very good county for villages is Wiltshire. Lacock is a prize specimen with both fine stone and timber-framed houses from the fifteenth century onwards. Sir William Sharington transformed the abbey buildings into a house distinguished for the early influence of the Renaissance within it, as also upon his tomb in the church. A living memory is that of W. H. Fox Talbot who here made the discoveries that led to instantaneous photography. One used to see the relics of his experiments in an upper room until the family relinquished their ancestral house, and these are now excellently displayed in the Fox Talbot Museum close by. Pretty villages decorate the valleys running down from the west to the Wiltshire Avon, such as Broad Chalke, beloved of artists, where the exquisite Queen Anne house in the middle was the home of Christopher Wood, the painter, then of photographer Cecil Beaton.

A different, practically perfect West Country village is Dunster in Somerset: dark blood-red sandstone in a magnificent situation between overhanging hills and woods; priory church, market cross, several medieval houses – of which the Luttrell Arms was an abbot's residence. All benevolently presided over by the castle, with its mound and towers, and gardened terraces.

At the other end of the country, in Cheshire, let us choose Gawsworth, situated around a green with a pond, several manor-sized houses. All this is black-and-white timbering country. The rectory provides a good specimen; so also the Hall, which was the home of the Fittons. Thus the notorious Mary Fitton appears as a girl on her parents' monument in the church. Her career is quite well known. She had auburn hair and grey-blue eyes, as one sees from her portraits at lovely Arbury – an exquisite house near Nuneaton, with incomparable Gothick fan-vaulting. That neighbourhood has been immortalized in literature by George Eliot, who was brought up there.

Right on the Scottish borders is unique Blanchland, an enclosed square with gates north and south. When I saw it forty years ago I thought it excellent defence against border incursions – some places in that part of the country (another is Penrith) were provided with a large central square, refuge for their cattle, and narrow defensible entrances to the town. So, too, many houses had their peel-tower to resort to for defence – like Yanwath near Carlisle, or Embleton vicarage in Northumberland where the historian Mandell Creighton wrote his books.

The enclosed square of Blanchland village, Northumberland, a refuge for the surrounding population when raids from across the Scottish border occurred in medieval times.

These timbered houses of Chilham in Kent stand in the square near the ancient castle.

Down south one thinks of Groombridge in Kent, with moated house, or Chilham with castle, church and hostelry, or Cobham with splendid seventeenth-century mansion and a chancel full of medieval brasses. In Sussex there is Burwash, with its well-proportioned iron-masters' houses in the street; Kipling's Jacobean house, Batemans, is down in the meadows below. Sussex has been much celebrated by the poets; here is John Drinkwater:

> For peace, than knowledge more desirable,
> Into your Sussex quietness I came.

Belloc, too, was very appreciative in both verse and prose. One of his best books, *The Four Men*, describes a long tramp the length of Sussex, with suitable diversions in country pubs on the road.

Above all there is Kipling:

> God gives all men all earth to love,
> But, since man's heart is small,
> Ordains for each one spot shall prove
> Beloved over all.
> Each to his choice, and I rejoice
> The lot has fallen to me
> In a fair ground — in a fair ground —
> Yea, Sussex by the sea!

Sussex proved an inspiration, an induction – for an Anglo-Indian, born and formed in India – to an earlier, secret England, full of a lost magic that spoke to a poet's imagination and which only he could express.

> See you our little mill that clacks,
> So busy by the brook?
> She has ground her corn and paid her tax
> Ever since Domesday Book.

The Dorset village of Milton
Abbas with the thatched
cottages which are a feature of
that part of the country.

In prose the impact led to *Puck of Pook's Hill* with its inspired sense of the past.

The present poet laureate, Sir John Betjeman, has strokes all round the wicket: Cornwall –
St Enodoc, St Cadoc's, St Ervan; Wantage, or Upper Lambourne, or North Oxford. For
suburban places speak to him equally: Harrow-on-the-Hill, or Camberley, or Letchworth.
Indeed we must not forget pioneering efforts in suburban amenities, like the Hampstead
Garden Suburb, or the delightful planned community of Whiteley Village in Surrey,
benefaction of a self-made millionaire when the going was good. Nor should one omit the
many well designed council-housing estates put up in the hopeful days after the First World
War. I think of those on the edges of the Morrells' park coming down from Headington into
Oxford, or along the road out of Tiverton down the lovely valley of the Exe.

Perhaps we should regard these planned communities as successors of the beautiful, if
uniform, villages erected away from the mansions of their owners, with their discriminating
aristocratic taste – such pretty villages as Nuneham Courtenay in Oxfordshire, or Milton
Abbas in Dorset.

 # 4 DEFENCES AND DWELLINGS

WINDSOR CASTLE PRESENTS THE IMAGE people regard as most representative of the country's historic heritage, more than any other – more even than the Houses of Parliament, Westminster Abbey or the Tower of London. Perhaps especially in the age of air-travel: departing or arriving, one gets a bird's-eye view of it all, a greeting or a farewell.

Where those places are confined to their particular function, Windsor Castle is complex and expresses several; and it presents much of the panorama of British history. Moreover, it is still going, still carries out its age-old functions – unlike similar sites, the Louvre or Versailles, Escorial or Winter Palace. Windsor has served continuously as royal residence, and fortress; St George's Chapel is a kind of 'cathedral', as it was often called in the eighteenth century, shrine of the Order of the Garter with its stalls and decorative crests and coats-of-arms. In the lowest court are the residents of the Knights of Windsor, retired servants of the Crown.

Parts of the buildings reflect what Britain's heritage owes to France: for much of the Middle Ages the royal house was French, the governing class a French military aristocracy. Edward III's Order of the Garter was inspired by the ideas of chivalry and the Arthurian legend of the Round Table. Young king James I of Scotland was confined here, fell in love with Joan Beaufort, was married to her and wrote *The King's Quair* to celebrate it.

The buildings still speak to us of art-loving Henry III. His father, King John, resided here during the time when he was forced to accept Magna Carta by the barons down in the meadows at Runnymede below. St George's Chapel is Edward IV's. Tudor monarchs have left their traces: Henry VII in a tower of the upper bailey, Henry VIII in a gateway, broad like himself, Elizabeth I in a slim gallery now the royal library. In her reign there took shape here a valuable work on education, her tutor Roger Ascham's book, *The Schoolmaster*.

Charles II loved the place and rebuilt much of the upper bailey, with a rich baroque chapel for his impartial devotions. He laid out the terraces and planted the Great Avenue. Much of his building was swept away in the reconstruction of the castle by George IV. He thought that the nation which had won Waterloo required something splendid, and – with the soul (and temperament) of an artist – he inspired it. We owe to him the raising of the Round Tower to dominate the whole – the *point d'appui*, with enormous flag flying, which we see across the lower Thames Valley. His was the idea of the Waterloo Chamber where so many state banquets have been held, and of Sir Thomas Lawrence's state-portraits of the potentates of that glorious time.

Naturally a place going for so long has its more morose memories – of the Civil War, which dispersed so many treasures of Crown and Church, regalia, pictures, vestments, objects of art and beauty. Cromwell's army held its decisive meeting here, which dealt suitably with the Levellers. Charles I was brought prisoner before his execution; the body, with the severed head, was transported back to rest in his own bedroom, before the procession of the snow-covered coffin to the chapel for the silent burial – the Puritans would not allow the touching prayer book service.

Our time has contributed another memory: the abdication of another uncompromising monarch, who yet loved Windsor and is buried here. The place has proved well able to absorb these shocks, and register their memories. It stands there, as one looks up from the playing-fields of Eton below, a symbol not only of the richness and variety of British history but of its continuity, of what silts up and endures – like a coral reef – when so much decays, perishes and vanishes.

At opposite poles, north and south, are the vast, Windsor-like symbols of Alnwick and Arundel Castles. Throughout the Middle Ages Alnwick, under the Percys, stood on guard against the Scots – and along the parapet of the barbican are armed figures warding them off. The castle has a dramatic position above its river, park ducally landscaped by 'Capability' Brown. Within, all kinds of treasures, portraits – one of the Wizard Earl who, with Ralegh

Previous pages Warwick Castle seen from the Castle Bridge.

Left The Round Tower at Windsor Castle. Dating originally from about 1272, it was heightened by George IV.

and other wits, turned the Tower of London into a scientific seminary under James I – relics of Charles I and Cromwell (whom the Percys supported), books and manuscripts galore. Arundel Castle has a similar situation above its river, and offers a comparable skyline in the southern landscape. Within are portraits and treasures of the Howard Dukes of Norfolk, and in the parish church a splendid series of their monuments and those of the Arundel earls from whom the castle came to them.

A number of castles are still inhabited. I think of charming Shirburn, a moated medieval and seventeenth-century place: a whole roomful of original Stubbses, the horses and grooms of the family; upstairs a library with a couple of Caxtons; beneath, an archive of scientific correspondence of the age of Newton and John Ray. Or Powderham in Devon, with charming music room and libraries *en suite* of the connoisseur William Courtenay. Or Rockingham behind its walls up above the forest; within, mementoes of Dickens who played in the private theatricals of the family and put the place into *Bleak House*. Or Powys, on the Welsh border, of rose-red stone, looming above its terraced gardens. Farnham Castle, of the bishops of Winchester, looks down upon that endearing Georgian High Street; Hartlebury and Rose Castles housed the bishops of Worcester and Carlisle.

Where is one to stop? Perhaps with Balmoral, that expression of Coburg romanticism, in the countryside that reminded Prince Albert of his native heath, Rosenau. Scotland has its still inhabited castles, mostly ducal: exquisite Drumlanrig of the Buccleuchs, Inverary (in a situation of breath-taking, if rainy, beauty) of the Argylls, Dunrobin of the Sutherlands. Culzean in its spectacular situation on the edge of its raw Ayrshire cliff – all sophisticated Adam within – has its memento of the Second World War, for here a flat was fitted up for the Allied commander-in-chief, Eisenhower, on his rare visits.

Coming a long way south to Severn country is Berkeley, exterior complete and little changed, interior enriched by many acquisitions in its restoration, upon which a fortune was spent in our time. Nothing extinguishes the sinister memory of Edward II, done to death here, and buried in Gloucester cathedral in a tomb that is a miracle of medieval art. For me

Below The terraced gardens at Powis Castle, in Wales, looking out from its almost impregnable position over the Welsh hills.

Right Berkeley Castle, Gloucestershire. Edward II was murdered there in 1327.

Caernarvon Castle in North Wales, built by Edward I in 1284.

the church has an extra association: a canon here in Richard II's time was John of Trevisa, an associate of Wyclif in translating the Bible and a formative maker of early English prose.

A contribution of our own age to the nation's inheritance is astonishing Castle Drogo in Devon, looking like some Scottish eyrie, but against the more coloured background of Dartmoor. Here is a Lutyens masterpiece, of precision, strength and mottled beauty of stone, 1000 feet up above the gorge of the Teign. All hail to Mr Drew of the Home and Colonial Stores, who made a rapid fortune when the going was good, and had the imagination to spend it in this memorable way, selecting Lutyens for his architect and himself pacing out the spectacular approach over the brow of that Dartmoor heath.

Many more ruined castles exist all over the country, all with different points of interest. For they fall into various categories, and succumbed to ruin in different ways. Little is left of Pontefract, a vast fortress like a Windsor of the north, it was so hammered by siege in the Civil War. It had its tragic memory too – of the murder of Richard II, no one knows how. Middleham, that frowning pile, has the appropriate memory of sinister, frowning Richard III, with his habit of biting his lip in tension.

Many castles were casualties of the Civil War, or 'slighted' by Parliamentary order afterwards to discourage royalists. Of such are Corfe in Dorset and Wardour in Wiltshire, both renowned for the prolonged fight they put up. Magnificent Raglan in Monmouthshire still bears evidence of the sophisticated taste of King Charles's time in the classical niches for statues and sculpture along the terrace – just the kind of thing Puritans hated. A still larger type of castle was that which Edward I built to enclose the Welsh: Caernarvon, where Edward II – Edward of Caernarvon – was born; Pembroke, where Henry VII was brought up as a boy, last hope of the Lancastrians, by his canny uncle, Jasper Tudor. Harlech endured a pitiful long siege for the sake of Owen Glendower, heroic spirit of Welsh resistance to the overbearing English.

Centres of royal territories were Clitheroe of the duchy of Lancaster, or Knaresborough and Wallingford, oddly enough, of the duchy of Cornwall. Within Cornwall three such eloquent ruins remain: Launceston and Trematon, guarding the entrances across the River Tamar, and romantic Restormel on its mound above the Fowey. This last was built originally by Henry III's brother, Richard, King of the Romans – the revenues from his lands enabled him to purchase the title and the succession to the Holy Roman (but German) Empire he did

Below right The ruins of Corfe Castle in Dorset. It was besieged by the Parliamentarians in 1646, after which it was dismantled and wrecked.

not attain through natural inheritance. Later, the Black Prince came this way *en route* to his duchy of Aquitaine, to Crécy and Poitiers and his wars in Spain.

A more endearing memory is that formidable North Country lass, Anne Clifford, Countess of Dorset, Pembroke and Montgomery, who found her extravagant South Country husbands so unsatisfactory. Retiring to the north, she enjoyed her widowhood much more, spending her large revenues on repairing and keeping her numerous habitations, Skipton, Brougham and Brough, Appleby where one remembers her best, and those Clifford tombs in the church at the foot of the street. Not afraid of standing up to Oliver Cromwell, a gentler side is to be seen in the memorial she put up to her tutor, Samuel Daniel, in the church of Beckington, beautiful Somerset village with its grey manor houses, Elizabethan and later. Daniel was well worthy to be thus commemorated: one of the best of Elizabethan writers, poet and historian, in spirit close to Shakespeare, whom he well knew, for he was the brother-in-law of John Florio, Southampton's Italian tutor. How these things come together!

A last category are those castles which were built by Henry VIII to defend the south coast. Such are Pendennis and St Mawes, on either side of Falmouth haven: the latter in the shape of three perfect lobes, with gun-emplacements and long inscription around its neck to the greater glory of Henry. Pendennis sustained a protracted siege in the cause of Charles I – heroic old John Arundell marching out with his company starving and the 'honours' of war. Way up the coast Walmer Castle has more recent memories, of the younger Pitt, but mostly of Wellington who loved residing here – one sees the chair in which he died, full of years and fame. Official residence of the Wardens of the Cinque Ports – the five ancient ports of Dover, Hastings, Romney, Hythe and Sandwich – the castle was not much frequented by Winston Churchill, he was so devoted to his own creation, Chartwell.

MOST ENGLISH PEOPLE'S IDEA of a palace is probably Buckingham Palace, with the royal standard floating over Aston Webb's Edwardian front, when the sovereign is in residence; and with the vast Queen Victoria Memorial in front – which 'Saki' Munro called the *Grossmutter Denkmal* in his brilliant fantasy, *When William Came*.

Actually Buckingham Palace's association with the Crown is not very long – it goes back only to George III. It is not the most historic or the most beautiful of royal residences, though the garden-front has the distinction of being by Nash, and the opulent interior is packed with treasures, Regency furniture, Meissen and the portraits of the Hanoverians' German relations.

The older English monarchs, Tudors and Stuarts, lived at Whitehall, which burned down in 1694, and at St James's, familiar from the Henry VIII gateway looking up St James's Street, of all those clubs. William III transferred himself to Kensington, which he largely built (the Kaiser gave his statue in front of the palace). William also added largely on to Hampton Court, commissioning Wren to build the brick fronts and courts; most of the Tudor building, including the great hall, is Henry VIII's, who took over from Wolsey, with his cultivated Renaissance tastes.

Most splendid of English palaces is appropriately a naval establishment: Greenwich. It was a favourite residence of Elizabeth I, who was born there; she died at Richmond, of which only fragments remain amid Queen Anne terraces, such as Maids-of-Honour Row. The royal palaces fell into decay with the Civil War and the austere Commonwealth – though Protector Oliver lived in some state at Whitehall and Hampton Court. Charles I, greatest of English art-collectors – most of whose acquisitions the Puritans sold off abroad – commissioned Inigo Jones to build the perfect Queen's House at Greenwich: along with his Banqueting House at Whitehall (from a window of which Charles I stepped out to his execution), the first completely classic masterpiece in England. After the Restoration Wren was called in to rebuild, and has bequeathed us that marvellous Greenwich river-front with

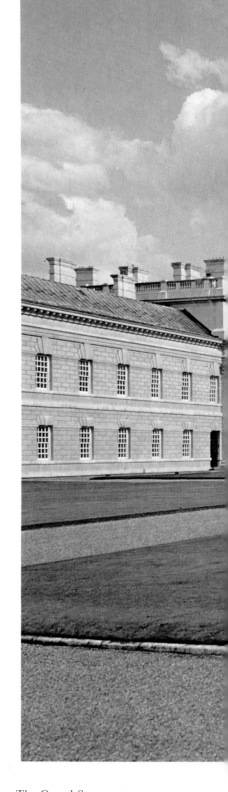

The Grand Square at Greenwich, showing in the background the Queen's House, commissioned by Charles I and built by Inigo Jones. Other parts were built by Sir Christopher Wren.

its cupolas: the masterpiece of his later period as St Paul's is of his earlier.

The Restoration was responsible also for Holyrood – like Charles II and James II (who lived there when ruling Scotland and suppressing irrepressible Covenanters), mainly French in character. So also was Hamilton Palace, unforgivably destroyed in our time: it would have made the ideal museum for the rich collections of works of art the Glasgow ship-owner, Sir William Burrell, brought together. Now one sees the grand fire-places and marble chimney-pieces in the Metropolitan Museum in New York.

This brings us to ducal palaces. I suppose everybody's first idea of a ducal palace is Blenheim, of the Churchills. They could hardly do better. When one first catches sight of it from Duchess Sarah's gateway, that spreading architectural scene in the distance like the back-drop in a theatre, one realizes that Vanbrugh was a dramatist as well as an architect.

Again, in the fantastic roofscape reflected in 'Capability' Brown's crescent-shaped lake, one senses a romantic vein amid so much classicism. The palace was indeed the fantasy – the Duchess called it the 'weakness' – of the most brilliant and daring of English soldiers, Marlborough. He set up Louis XIV's head upon his garden-front, and this was John Churchill's answer to Versailles, no less than the Battle of Blenheim the palace commemorates. It was paid for by a grateful nation – the nation has even more reason to be grateful to his descendant, Sir Winston (the Duke's father was the first Sir Winston); it was always intended not only as a family residence but as a monument to the military glory of the nation that defeated Louis XIV.

Blenheim is built of a honey-coloured stone that takes on all golden hues from lemon to darkest orange; Vanbrugh's Castle Howard in Yorkshire is of rose and cream stone, integrated by the central feature of a dome. Wentworth Woodhouse of Lord Rockingham – who, supporting the colonial cause, as most Whigs did, repealed the Stamp Act to please the Americans – has the longest front in England. Chatsworth, in its Derbyshire parkland with a cascade like the waters of Tivoli, can hardly be smaller. Badminton of the Beauforts, Holkham of the Leicesters, Longleat of the Baths, Kedleston of the Curzons, Burghley and Hatfield of the Exeters and Salisburys, Boughton of the Buccleuchs, Hopetoun of the Linlithgows are all vast, as were Eaton Hall of the Westminsters and Trentham of the Sutherlands.

The gardens at Blenheim, of 20th century design, look out over the lake created by 'Capability' Brown.

The ducal palace of Blenheim, near the village of Woodstock in Oxfordshire,
is one of Vanbrugh's grandest creations.

Longleat House, in Wiltshire, home of the
Marquis of Bath, and now containing a Safari Park
in its grounds.

These palaces form one of the noblest provinces in the heritage of the nation; they incorporate, they incarnate, they carry with them a considerable part of the national story – in particular the Revolution of 1688. The grandees, not only Whig, were behind that decisive event; their political power and ability (James II was a fool to challenge a confrontation) are expressed in the grandeur of their buildings and the landscapes they planned and laid out.

These places have fascinating variety. Longleat is the nearest the Elizabethans got to a symmetrical Renaissance palace – in that lovely landscape (now sporting lions for the people!). Within are memories to occupy the mind – Bishop Ken's library at the top of the house, all those manuscripts and papers. The possessions of Chatsworth were hardly credible: pictures and portraits in hundreds, though the rare collection of the Elizabethan drama is now in the Huntington Library in California, like the Ellesmere treasures (the Ellesmere Chaucer, with portrait of the poet, is Britain's main medieval literary manuscript) and all the papers from Stowe, of the Grenvilles, Dukes of Buckingham. No palace is more a temple of the leading Whig figures than Stowe – one of the many garden temples which are a feature of that vast lay-out is dedicated to these spirits, John Hampden, Sir John Eliot, John Milton and all the other Whig Johnnies.

Badminton, façade ornate with cupolas, is indubitably Tory: it puts its foot heavily down. After all the sacrifices of that family for the Stuarts, there is even, understandably, a Jacobite inflexion. Boughton, of the Montagus – inherited with two other dukedoms by the lucky Buccleuchs – is Whig, but nevertheless French in inspiration. Ralph Montagu, a Revolution duke, was a well remunerated ambassador to Louis XIV; he added an exquisite French *château* to an already large Elizabethan house, and filled it with the finest Louis XIV furniture that exists. Haddon Hall, of the Rutlands, takes us back to the Middle Ages, with rising

The State Drawing Room at Chatsworth House, Derbyshire.

courts along those gardened terraces, upon which an Elizabethan gallery looks out. Kedleston, also in Derbyshire, has a noble front with a marble hall as big as a railway station hall (so has Holkham); in addition to this Adam built half of a crescent garden-front, more imaginative and exquisite. If it had ever been finished, it would have loomed as large as Blenheim.

ABROAD are larger and grander palaces: what is more characteristic of the English scene is the country-house. An informed judgment would agree that English country-house life exemplified in its day the best and most balanced kind of any in the world. For one thing, it held a proper balance between country and town; between country air and pursuits, occupations and sports, and sophisticated urban standards and tastes; between agriculture, horticulture, planting of woods and parks and avenues, draining marsh and creating lakes on the one hand, and the paintings, furnishings and books they encouraged and acquired from the capital. Moreover, the country-houses all over the land, in every properly constituted parish, stood above all for *responsibility*, a responsible attitude towards people locally and on a county basis, and towards society at large.

No wonder this society was the most satisfactory and successful society in the world, as societies go – and its achievements all over the outside world have left their evidences from New England to India, from Canada and Cathay to New Zealand.

A properly regulated parish had, as its core, the squire's house, church and parsonage: the

The fine Elizabethan gallery looking out over the gardened terraces of Haddon Hall in Derbyshire.

116

The Palladian bridge in the grounds of Wilton House in Wiltshire, which is famous for the work done there in the seventeenth century by Inigo Jones and John Webb.

squire and parson ruled it for its good. (Naturally there were good and bad squires, even good and bad parsons.) On a county basis the country gentry foregathered, judicially at quarter-sessions and assizes, later at county council meetings, aided by their professional advisers, the lawyers. Socially, they met at their assemblies: every provincial capital had its assembly rooms, like Bath or York – even little Truro had its own, of which only the exquisite façade, in Ralph Allen's Bath stone, remains. On a national basis the ruling class met in Parliament: it had the political genius of Walpoles, Pitts, Foxes and Cannings at its disposal. English society was always more mobile and flexible than others – actually less snobbish than French or Italian or German – and was ever ready to recruit outsiders like Burke or Disraeli, let alone a Peel or a Gladstone.

All this is evident to the informed eye in the houses they lived in – even the radical Gladstone moved to a castle, Hawarden; Disraeli was equipped with country-house and estate at Hughenden; the Irishman Burke lived generously, on credit and in debt, at a country-house near Beaconsfield.

One cannot do justice to these houses that once existed in thousands all over the country, and have been and are being destroyed in hundreds in our time. (The proper thing is to find alternative uses for this irreplaceable heritage.) They were, along with the churches, and the landscapes of which they were often sited to be the focal points, what was most characteristic of and special to the English scene.

Here one can only pick and choose, perhaps best in some chronological fashion.

Note that these houses, from the Middle Ages onwards, vary in scale as well as in regional character from quasi-castles like noble Penshurst in Kent to exquisite Lytes Cary in Somerset, or from delicious Nether Lyppiatt in the Cotswolds to tiny Tonacombe in north Cornwall, with diminutive hall and minstrels' gallery. Penshurst has a grand fourteenth-century hall and armoury, an Elizabethan gallery full of the Sidneys, for the overwhelming memory here is of Philip Sidney. His sister, the Countess of Pembroke, who published his

In its beautiful setting in a 'bowl' of the Warwickshire hills, Compton Wynyates was built in the fifteenth century and remains virtually unchanged.

Arcadia, lived at the Elizabethan Wilton. This was transformed in the next generation to the most perfect of Caroline houses, by the genius of Inigo Jones and John Webb, with a magnificent saloon and decorated rooms, sculpture, paintings, Palladian bridge and all. But is this not rather a palace?

Of medieval houses Wiltshire has its complement, notably Great Chalfield, as Dorset has Athelhampton. But I shall choose Compton Wynyates in Warwickshire for completeness and perfection in its fittings, down to shutters with iron hasps and hinges, and for its setting in that bowl of the hills: one looks down upon it from all round the rim with unspeakable delight and inexpressible thoughts of Lancastrians and Yorkists, Cavaliers and Parliamentarians chasing across the Warwickshire countryside Shakespeare so loved – and all the while the country life going forward that he knew so well, christenings and churchings, bowls on the green, markets and fairs and sheep-shearings as in *The Winter's Tale*. Perhaps it is winter itself,

> *When icicles hang by the wall,*
> *And Dick, the shepherd, blows his nail,*
> *And Tom bears logs into the hall,*
> *And milk comes frozen home in pail . . .*

It is impossible to categorize St Michael's Mount, for it is unique. The nucleus of it is medieval, the church with attendant chapel, where an archpriest and a couple of canons kept their vigil and tended the light warning ships off those reefs and sands, beneath which is a buried wood. Hence its old name, Carrick-loose-en-coose, the grey rock in the wood. After the Reformation defence came to the fore: the archpriest was succeeded by the captain and a posse of soldiers:

> *Where the great vision of the guarded Mount*
> *Looks towards Namancos and Bayona's hold.*

After the Civil War it came happily into the possession of the St Aubyns. The Elizabethans

Above St Michael's Mount, in Cornwall, is joined to the mainland by a natural causeway which is passable only at low tide. The Chapel of St Michael, pictured here, is of fifteenth-century construction, and topped with battlements.

had turned the hall into a dining-room, with plaster frieze of Chevy Chase – beloved of Sidney – for cornice. The eighteenth century turned chapels into Gothick drawing-rooms; the nineteenth made it into something like a castle. It always was a place of pilgrimage; modern tourists are the successors of the pilgrims.

Of all Elizabethan houses I choose Hardwick in Derbyshire, tall, with its many-windowed 'walls of glass', the place afire with the westering sun upon them all; fantastic sky-line with six turrets towering above it – one of them the room of the philosopher Hobbes for many years. The top storey is the grandest: Presence Chamber with deep chivalric frieze, one of the loveliest rooms in Europe, the prime Elizabethan colours throughout now faded to pale moonlight shades. A long gallery for walking and talking was a feature of most mansions built at this time: here presides the portrait of Bess of Hardwick whose creation it was, surrounded by the Stuart relations she recruited to her family.

With Sarah Churchill with whom she had much in common, Bess was one of the foremost of English women: above all in business ability and ambition. The daughter of a small squire,

Below The magnificent Gallery at Hardwick Hall in Derbyshire, built by Elizabeth ('Bess') of Hardwick after the death of her last husband in 1591. On the left-hand side of the photograph is a painting of Bess of Hardwick.

Right This detail from an embroidery at Hardwick shows contemporary costume.

she made her career by four ascending marriages, ending with the first peer in the kingdom and making herself the ancestress of three dukedoms. She aimed further. When a presumptive heir to the Stuarts came to Hardwick he did not get away without marrying one of her daughters. The result was little Arabella Stuart, next heir to the throne after James I – one sees the bedroom inside her grandmother's, where this precious possession was safeguarded. *La carriere ouverte aux talents* (a career open to one's talents) could apply in the age of Elizabeth I to women as well as men.

I am not forgetting Montacute, even more beautiful in the colouring of its stone with pretty garden pavilions along the terrace such as Elizabethans loved – Elizabeth I had one at the end of the terrace she built at Windsor. Or Wollaton near Nottingham, with its skyscraping hall thrusting up through the centre, towers at the corners, all expressive of the soaring fantasy and ambition of the age which went into other comparable works: Spenser's *Faerie Queene*, Ralegh's thrusting career or his *History of the World*, or Drake's unparalleled voyage around it.

Scores of smaller Elizabethan houses bespeak domestic comfort – that is what is really characteristic of them. Grander palaces abroad, the Palazzo Colonna or the Palazzo Doria in Rome, have vaster halls and galleries, but nowhere comfortable for the private life. Private comfort, domesticity, were provided for in English country-houses, however large: even in a palace like Hatfield a wing with its own staircase gives comfortable quarters for the family. (Nowadays a flat often serves.) All the same, there is an optimum for a country-house – say, something of medium size and perfect proportions, like Kingston Russell in Dorset, from which that prodigious family came.

No houses are more livable than those built from the Restoration onwards, in the idiom of Wren and Gibbs, though some of these are palatial. None is more completely satisfying than Belton, of the Brownlows, near Grantham – and someone of that fortunate family had recorded upon a tombstone the joy to be found in living in that place. The charming village setting bespeaks no less the care and forethought for dependents and tenantry, as in so many places. Aynho, of the Cartwrights in Northamptonshire, is an example of this, with regular houses and cottages in that good iron-stone, all planted with fruit-trees. Who but a squire of the place would have the attentive care to plant fruit-trees along the walls?

Of the seventeenth century I think of Brympton D'Evercy in Somerset, with its chaste Caroline front looking from its terrace down to the pool. Not long ago it still possessed the family treasures, including a portrait of the dead Monmouth; for in this house of the Whig Scropes he spent a night on his way to Sedgemoor. The comparable front of Lamport in Northamptonshire was the work of Webb for the Ishams. They were a bookish family; among their books was an invaluable collection of Shakespeare quartos – worth a million but sold for a pittance by the Victorians and now in the Huntington Library in California.

The seventeenth-century house of Brympton D'Evercy in Somerset.

Althorp of the Spencers and Petworth of the Wyndhams are of the later seventeenth century. The former was put into a state of perfection by the late earl, a connoisseur. It contains many of the possessions of Sarah Marlborough, including her gold plate – one of the few English houses where there was gold plate to eat off, though plenty had exquisite silver. A large gallery of portraits contained a similar collection of the 'Windsor Beauties' – Lelys and Knellers of those strange ladies, extremely *décolleté*, displaying their full-bosomed charms. Petworth is of this period – but again a palace. The celebrated Earl of Egremont did his duty for the nation's heritage, if not for his family. All his children were illegitimate, but he supported artists like Turner for years, while the latter painted his glorious pictures of house and park.

With Queen Anne and the Georges, the eighteenth and early nineteenth centuries, comes the heyday of the country-houses. All over England, and to a lesser extent southern Scotland and Wales – equally notably in Ireland, though that is out of bounds for the purposes of this book – older houses were being reconstructed, new mansions built, parks created to surround them. Where to begin or end? I shall select only a few, for their perfection, their significance, or what they have to tell us.

My impression is that, generally speaking, Northamptonshire and Norfolk have the finest among the larger country-houses, though we have seen that Yorkshire and Derbyshire have their palaces. Kirby Hall is the most lovely of ruined houses, part Elizabethan, part Caroline, its coupled bays having come to rest, as Sacheverell Sitwell says, like galleons in the level Northamptonshire fields. Boughton, Althorp and Deene Park are not far; and there is Drayton – medieval, Elizabethan, and William-and-Mary – with historic furniture and the china collected by Lady Betty Germain, Swift's friend.

Norfolk has palaces: vast Holkham, with an imperial entrance-hall like something in Rome. Elizabethan Blickling is by Robert Lyming, Robert Cecil's architect for Hatfield; one

Turner's view of Petworth House 'Dewy Morning', which hangs in the house.

recognizes similar features, especially the staircase. A friend tells me that most strictly beautiful is Houghton – paradoxical that coarse Sir Robert Walpole should have been an aesthete: it convinces one that Horace must have been his son after all. All that his idiot of a grandson could do was to sell Sir Robert's marvellous collection of pictures to Catherine the Great, and their remainder now graces the Hermitage.

Attingham in Shropshire I choose for perfection: designed by George Steuart, columned portico, colonnaded wings – the eighteenth century could hardly go wrong, such were the standards of taste, and sense of proportion. The interior was even improved by Nash: delicious decoration and all its original furniture, gilt and otherwise. In the eighteenth century the best standards were promulgated from the capital: only a dozen or so patterns of mouldings for cornices, dados, door-cases, etc., were disseminated from the centre. Hence people could hardly go wrong.

Antony in Cornwall looks like a Gibbs house: the design could have come out of Gibb's book, for books of patterns – such as Serlio's earlier – had been circulated among connoisseurs (like Lord Burghley) from the Elizabethan Age onwards. Antony is built of cream-coloured stone, with dove-grey and lavender mottlings; a rich interior of dark woodwork and panelling, graced with the books of scholar-ancestors, on both Carew and Pole sides. A little earlier is Sudbury of the Vernons, in Derbyshire: rich red stone outside, decorative Caroline interiors – never shall I forget the cedar-shaded, green summer light filtering in at the end of the long gallery.

Most of all should I like to inhabit Uppark, high on its plateau above Petersfield – Edward Gibbon country – looking across to the shipping of the Solent. That shapely house of the Featherstonhaughs has an unchanged interior, all the elegancies of Regency furniture, books, pictures; and below stairs the inelegant memory of H. G. Wells, the housekeeper's son, no aesthete, who aimed a shot at one of the pictures.

Wallington is a favourite of mine for its associations, though it is also a piece of sophisticated architecture, inside and out, planted on the gaunt Northumberland plateau, not far from Otterburn of the ballads, looking towards the Cheviots. Within, the courtyard was roofed over to make an Italian *cortile* in high Victorian style, with frescoes under Ruskin's influence. The tradition of the house under the Trevelyans was high Whig. Sir George Otto Trevelyan, in his classic *History of the American Revolution*, thought that the Americans could

do nothing wrong and George III nothing right. The deities of the house are Charles James Fox and Macaulay, whose sister married Sir Charles Trevelyan, greatest of civil servants, who reformed Indian administration and introduced competitive examination for entrance to the Civil Service. Charles James Fox's set of counters is there, with which he gambled away a fortune – no wonder the conscientious George III did not want to put *him* in charge of the Treasury!

There are perfect Regency interiors at Berrington, by Henry Holland, in Shropshire, and Heveningham, by James Wyatt, in Suffolk. I confess to a preference for Robert Adam: never have I seen such interiors as Syon – the delicacy and richness of those ceilings; the decoration of the long Elizabethan library, with its pale blues faded to the colour of a spring sky; the footmen's waiting hall with the gold-topped scagliola columns fished up from the bed of the Tiber – fourteen of them! The neighbouring Osterley Park is hardly less entrancing, Adam's decoration again set within an Elizabethan exterior. At Kenwood he designed the whole, for the eminent jurist, Lord Mansfield, up at Hampstead, since an idiot mob had burned his magnificent library down in London (as another mob did Joseph Priestley's library in Birmingham). These houses may, however, be thought of as suburban, though rural enough in their surroundings when built. And in fact one thinks of Regency architecture as essentially urban – the columned terraces of Nash in Carlton Gardens or around Regent's Park. He did, however, build so romantic a fantasy as Caerhays Castle in Cornwall.

We must confront the Victorians. An early Victorian house like Scotney Castle can be beautiful: underneath the Victorian Gothic, the proportions and shapes of the rooms are essentially Georgian. And this house, inspired by the scholarly connoisseurship of Christopher Hussey, has acquired appropriate Victorian paintings.

The trouble with the Victorians was that they were so self-confident – they would pull down almost anything, especially if it was a Georgian church; and they were so restlessly experimental – they revelled in a-symmetry and would build in bricks of any texture, including a hard blue brick that looks more like metal. Kipling, who had a Pre-Raphaelite streak in him, said that this was why they liked monkey-puzzles – because they were the nearest thing to iron or metal-work in trees. There are Pre-Raphaelite houses, such as Wightwick near Wolverhampton, which have recognizable character. They are not the most

Left Robert Adam, famous **architect** and designer of the eighteenth century, spent three years in Italy studying Roman architecture. The Library at Kenwood in North London is characteristic of the distinctive style he developed.

Below The medieval ruin in the grounds of Scotney Castle in Kent, surrounded by a moat.

livable of houses – Kipling's Burwash interior, in the same mode, is positively uncomfortable, with oak settles and bare boards, nor are they wholly mitigated by Kempe glass, or Morris wallpapers and chintzes.

IT IS USUAL to point out a marked contrast between the preferences of the English aristocracy for living in the country and the French and Italian for life at Versailles or in Paris, while the Italians preferred their *palazzi* in the city with villas in the country. In Britain it was the other way round. All the same there were very fine town-houses, especially in London. Many of the grandest of these have gone. Lansdowne House stood at the bottom of Berkeley Square; one reads about it in the letters of Matthew Arnold, and one can see its noble dining-room, in which the Earl of Shelburne, 'the Jesuit of Berkeley Square', gathered his pro-American friends and philosophical Radicals like Jeremy Bentham – in the Metropolitan Museum in New York. Jeremy himself may still be seen, stuffed and clothed at University College in Gower Street: the old tough survived the wartime bombing. Quite a number of good town-houses remain on the west side of Berkeley Square, with their decorative ironwork and shapely torch-extinguishers, like candle-snuffers, for the link-boys. How it brings back eighteenth-century life to the imagination!

Many of the grand town-houses have gone to make way for offices, hotels or blocks of flats: Norfolk House, Devonshire House, Londonderry House and large numbers in all the London squares. Some, however, remain. The most familiar to all, and most famous, is No. 1 Piccadilly, otherwise Apsley House, now islanded, the town residence of the Duke of Wellington and full of his best pictures and treasures: now a museum. He preferred living in town, with his eye on events and his part to play in them, to living at Stratfieldsaye – the beauty of which was enhanced in our time by the late duke, architect and connoisseur. (The hall has a splendid mosaic pavement from near-by Silchester, and busts of Wellington's colleagues against Napoleon, Alexander I, the handsome Nicholas I of Russia, and others.)

Among other large town-houses that remain are Derby House, north of Oxford Street, with noble staircase and suites of rooms; Chandos House near by; Hertford House which contains the wonderful French furniture, pictures and *objets d'art* of the Wallace Collection; or Chatham House, where subsequently Gladstone lived, now an Institute for International Affairs. Indeed, large numbers of distinguished town-houses of lesser size, with their varied decoration, plasterwork, woodwork and ironwork fortunately remain. Similarly in cities and towns all over the country, especially provincial capitals like Norwich, Bristol, Exeter, Nottingham, which had a noble procession of town houses all the way down from the castle to Low Pavement and up along High Pavement to St Mary's church with its Close; or Shrewsbury, which had an exceptional number of fine black-and-white Elizabethan houses. Hull, heavily bombed, once had streets of good houses; perhaps the best remains in Wilberforce House, now a museum in honour of the liberator of the slaves.

ALL THESE HOUSES in the country stood in their proper perspective of gardens, pleasure grounds, parks and plantations. How their creators viewed and discussed them may be read in Jane Austen's *Sense and Sensibility* or *Mansfield Park*; or seen in the coloured aquatints of William Gilpin's books on the picturesque.

Landscape gardening is properly an English creation, a development of Romanticism. One sees tribute paid to it in the number of 'English gardens' abroad, like that at Munich, or, most beautiful of all, that at Cintra near Lisbon. Before this gardens were formal and regular, usually symmetrical with central features, like architecture. Indeed, Elizabethan gardens were thought of as an extension of the house, green rooms and pleached alleys in which to walk sheltered from the weather. Elizabeth I often received visitors, discussed affairs or did business on such walks.

Such were the formal gardens, the beds laid out with intricate devices or knots – hence

Apsley House in London (No 1 Piccadilly), once the house of the Duke of Wellington. Today it houses a museum.

'knot-gardens' – which Francis Bacon discusses and makes suggestions for in his famous essay. He advised on the lay-out of the garden at Gray's Inn when he lived there. These gardens usually included an arbour for sitting out, and a mound for the pleasure of the ascent, from which to view the whole. One sees an eighteenth-century mound in the garden at New College, Oxford.

Numerous engravings, particularly those of Kip, paintings, even embroideries, stitch-work and *petit-point*, show one precisely what earlier formal gardens were like. Some of them, like that at the vast mansion Vanbrugh built for Bubb Doddington at Eastbury, Dorset, were magnificent. I cannot but regret the architectural garden Queen Anne's gardener, Wise, formed at Blenheim to carry out the military conception of the place: beyond the south front a walled garden in the form of a citadel, raised bastions, walks of various coloured stones, fountains, sculptures, and even flowers. 'Capability' Brown swept all that away for acres of plain sward, and on the other side gave us the romantic scenery of a lake. The Ninth Duke – Winston Churchill's cousin – compensated the loss (with Vanderbilt money) with the noblest formal garden created in England in our time: a water-garden, fountains, *pièces d'eau*, naiads and spouting tritons all down those terraces to the lake. All this is in the French taste – but how appropriate for the opposite number to Versailles; and how much the nation owes to that duke with the soul of an artist!

127

Earlier gardens went in for topiary work: clipping shrubs, particularly yew, into the form of animals, birds, kings and queens, lions, chess-men. A remarkable example remains at beautiful Levens in Cumbria. Another, of chess-men, has been preserved at Haseley Court in Oxfordshire by a talented Virginian lady who has re-created the garden and even rehabilitated the canal at its boundary. Formal garden canals came in with Dutch William: one sees evidences in them in disuse at Sir William Temple's Moor Park near Farnham – he spent years as ambassador in Holland.

Formal or informal, magnificent or small and endearing, with or without their proper houses to accompany them, the gardens and parks of England come to mind to carry the country's image when one is in exile, like the sound of church bells across the countryside. One thinks of the formal rides radiating from Worcester Lodge at the gateway to Badminton; the swathes cut through the woods at Bodnant, filled with the brilliant colours of rhododendron in spring; the falling lakes and grottoes of Stourhead; the terraces and temples of Rousham Park in Oxfordshire; the formal Italian garden and elegant Regency glass-houses at Bicton; the rare trees of Killerton, Knightshayes or Pencarrow; the vista across the lake from the eighteenth-century Gothick of Sheffield Park, where Gibbon lived with his friends, the Holroyds, to the mausoleum under the spire at the far end, where they all lie together. Or, again, the roses at Sissinghurst, the rare daffodils at Trewithen, the magnolias and tree ferns that surround Nash's romantic Caerhays Castle, the blue agapanthus at St Michael's Mount, lying like pools reflecting the blue of the sea.

I confess to a particular affection for the Physick Garden at Oxford, the first in England, within its Caroline walls, and its ornate gateway by Nicholas Stone: the whole place conceived and founded by Southampton's bachelor friend, Henry Danvers, under the shadow of Magdalen Tower, within the angle of the bridge and the flowing Thames.

Above The view across Sheffield Park lake in autumn.

Left One of Britain's specialities in the field of art is the landscape garden. Stourhead, in Wiltshire, started by Henry Hoare in 1714, and later worked on by 'Capability' Brown and Uvedale Price, is a perfect example of the style.

RELIGION AND EDUCATION are aspects of Britain's heritage which go together, since initially all through the Middle Ages and subsequent centuries up to yesterday, education was the prerogative of the Church. They are still closely connected in the public schools, the private foundations of the upper and middle classes. The Church is the nursing mother of us all, whatever our sect or denomination, even if we have none. Second, since my approach in this book is visual, I shall not be waffling about religion or education in general, but in concrete terms: I shall illustrate the theme from our cathedrals and churches, colleges, universities and schools.

Religion in England, even in Britain as a whole, has been dominantly practical: the word itself suggests a binding together in community. The British have not been much given to the mystical ecstasies of the Continent, or to the fanaticisms which have from time to time ravaged it. The emphasis has been on the moral rather than the metaphysical, on the practical and social. We might say that its outstanding figures in history have been teachers, preachers and organizers: St Boniface, who organized the Church in Germany, John Wesley who founded a world church, at any rate of the English-speaking world. Even the Celtic saints were teachers. St Augustine and Theodore of Tarsus were organizers and educators.

Their base was Canterbury. A flicker of Rome remained there in one or two early churches; later, St Augustine's monastery came almost to rival the cathedral in splendour: a victim of the Reformation, its foundations can be followed. The martyrdom of Archbishop Becket created a sensation all over Europe, so that St Thomas of Canterbury became the most popular of English saints abroad. His shrine brought honour and glory, and wealth, to the cathedral: one sees evidences still in the Corona, 'Becket's Crown', at the east end, and touchingly in the *graffiti* scratched on the walls, by pilgrims dedicating gifts, around the empty space where, till the Reformation, the shrine stood for veneration. Then there is the chapel where the murder took place – which should be restored as such.

Canterbury is the most complex of Britain's cathedrals: there is the Norman choir with its chapels, the double transepts, noble Perpendicular nave, cloister, chapter-house, library. It has retained a good deal of medieval glass, both early and late; in St Gabriel's Chapel have survived early frescoes of the highest artistic quality. The monuments record much of medieval history. Here is the Black Prince in full armour with knightly accoutrements, shield, helm, gauntlets; above him, stately tester with a representation of the Trinity, the festival which Becket ordained to be kept: we still keep it – it is the annual feast of my parish in Cornwall. Henry IV is here with his queen, Joan of Navarre: we see the thrusting,

Previous pages Canterbury Cathedral became a place of pilgrimage after the murder of Archbishop Thomas Becket on the steps of an altar in 1170.

Far left This window in the Water Tower is a fine example of the medieval stained-glass to be found in Canterbury Cathedral.

Left The tomb of the Black Prince, Edward, son and heir of Edward III, near the shrine to St Thomas Becket in Canterbury Cathedral. His helmet and shield hang above the fine portrait effigy.

This section of the Pilgrim's Way, near Charing in Kent, is a section of the route taken by medieval pilgrims from London to Canterbury.

bull-necked, apoplectic fellow he was. All round are the tombs of the archbishops, primates of the English church, including Chichele's, founder of All Souls College, which keeps his tomb in good fettle, in place of praying for his soul.

Besides all this the pilgrimage to Canterbury along the Pilgrims' Way is enshrined in the most endearing work of medieval literature, Chaucer's *Canterbury Tales*.

Many of the monastic buildings remain in the Close, nostalgically described by Walter Pater, in *Emerald Uthwart*. He was a boy at the King's School, which, as the archbishop's, must go right back to St Augustine and is thus the oldest in the kingdom. Its only rival is St Peter's at York, which goes back to the original school gathered round the archbishop there. Its most notorious pupil has entered even into English folklore: Guy Fawkes of Gunpowder Plot. An old Cotswold shepherd – as it might be out of *The Winter's Tale* – once told a friend of mine that he would be seventy 'come Gunpowder Day'. We still celebrate it with fireworks and crackers on 5 November; but it is not celebrated at St Peter's School, York.

We have already visited a number of cathedrals – some of them had their special rites and

'Uses' before the Reformation, notably Hereford and Durham. The Sarum Use, that is, Salisbury's, was fairly general over the south, and became the conservative basis of the prayer book of the eminent Cambridge liturgiologist, Archbishop Cranmer, Protestant martyr. (He had tried in vain to save his opposite number, Sir (now St) Thomas More, Catholic martyr.) At Old St Paul's Cathedral, in pre-Reformation days, there was a charming rite when they commemorated the feast by bringing the buck for it up to the high altar.

The Dean and Chapter being apparelled in copes and vestments, with garlands of roses on their heads, they sent the body of the buck to the baking and had the head fixed on a pole, borne before the Cross in their procession, until they issued out of the west door, where the keeper that brought it blowed the death of the buck. And then the horns that were about the City presently [i.e. immediately] answered him in like manner.

There followed dinner, and a distribution of groats (4d pieces – about 1½p). Evidently there is something to be said for 'Merrie England', before the time of the Puritans. It would have been amusing to see the celebrated 'Gloomy Dean' Inge, crowned with roses, or even Dean Donne, the poet, in that get-up.

Let us conclude our representation of English cathedrals with Ely for the east, and Exeter

Ely Cathedral, Cambridgeshire, on the Isle of Ely, is approached over water meadows. Founded by the first Norman abbot of Ely, Simeon, in the eleventh century, it dominates the surrounding countryside.

Above right The Norman north transept and the choir of Ely Cathedral, seen here from the elaborate central octagon.

for the west. Ely is a very grand affair, standing up like a vast ocean liner above the watery Fenland. Its unique outline, with immense west tower and elaborate central octagon, bulks largely on its eminence for miles around. In early days the waters were much more extensive and came right up to the fane:

Merrily sungen the monks in Ely
When Canute the king rowed by ...

We are reminded how much medieval music owed to the Church. I suppose that John Dunstable, the leading composer of the fifteenth century, whose fame extended all over Europe, was connected with Dunstable Priory. When the monasteries were dissolved, Henry VIII, who was a skilled musician – we still sing an anthem or two of his composing – took over the organist of Waltham Abbey, Thomas Tallis, for his Chapel Royal. Thus Tallis was able, as an Anglican, to compose not only Latin masses but to set the music for the new English Use which has continued to be sung to this day.

Exeter Cathedral has a couple of charming mementoes to the place of music in the Church. High up in the nave is a minstrels' gallery, a choir of angels sculpted, playing on their instruments; elsewhere a young Elizabethan organist is depicted with his organ, in relief upon a plaque full of feeling. Like Salisbury, Exeter is all of one piece, as one sees it approaching from the west, up on its hill dominating the city. Where Salisbury is chaste Early English, Exeter is Decorated, everything of marked richness, especially its array of sculpted bosses. All these things were made out of the sheer joy of creating. The bishop's throne here, of Edward II's reign, 'is the most exquisite piece of woodwork of its date in England and perhaps in Europe'. It survived the bombs of the German 'Baedeker raid' which fell upon the cathedral and severely damaged it, the city much worse. The grand effect is, on entering the west door, the long unbroken line of roof. The cathedral has a younger sister, built very much on its lines, in the collegiate church of Ottery St Mary. Here Alexander Barclay, a canon, indicted his English version of *The Ship of Fools*, a work prolific of progeny up to Katherine Anne Porter's novel in our time; also here some of the earliest English printing was accomplished.

HOLY TRINITY, Stratford-upon-Avon, gives us an example of a collegiate church: the chancel was that of a community of secular priests, not monks, who had their home in the college on the south side of it. In Shakespeare's time this belonged to his friends, the Combes.

Above The splendid collegiate Church of Beverley Minster, is on the site of a Saxon church founded by John of Beverley (640–721) in the East Riding of Yorkshire.

Left The fourteenth-century Exeter Cathedral is remarkable for its unbroken vaulted roof. Its west front, in Decorated style, is seen here.

Right The collegiate Holy Trinity Church, Stratford-upon-Avon, was once the home of a community of secular priests.

The most splendid collegiate church in the country is Beverley Minster, in Yorkshire, a kind of Westminster Abbey of the north – except that, where the abbey is French in design, Beverley is entirely English Perpendicular.

The tombs within offer a fine collection, though Westminster is an incomparable treasure-house of such from all periods – no country has such a Pantheon of its celebrities (non-celebrities too: these might be tactfully diminished, to make room). The Percy tomb at Beverley is a masterpiece of Decorated design and sculpture. Beneath the high altar here, as at York and Winchester, there is a holy well – to bring home to one the continuity of these sacred sites from pagan days. In the eighteenth century an architect of genius, Nicholas Hawksmoor – builder of the western towers of Westminster Abbey and of the Great Quadrangle at All Souls – did a remarkable job at Beverley: he levered back the whole wall of the north transept, dangerously leaning, into position. He erected a cupola at the crossing, and a stone rood-screen with Gothick figures. This was swept away by the Victorians, who regarded it as 'debased': plain proof that to them aesthetics were a department of ethics. They hated everything Georgian, and neglected Bath – one reason why it has remained providentially intact from them.

A fair number of monastic churches have come down to us intact, or partially, in use as parish churches. Among the former is magnificent Tewkesbury, which we owe to the local pride of those Tudor parishioners. It is now the glory of a lovely town, also unspoiled. In Hampshire we have Christchurch Priory and Romsey Abbey, with its famous Anglo-Saxon rood upon an outside wall. Some parishes preserved a portion of a church too large for them: at Pershore the exquisite Early English choir, at Malmesbury the Norman nave with the finest Romanesque portal in the country. Sometimes the monastic church itself was turned into a house – as at Buckland Abbey near Plymouth, transformed by the Grenvilles, purchased by Drake with the proceeds of his voyage round the world. The bulk went to the queen as chief investor; with what she left him he was able to buy Sheafhayne and Yarcombe manor.

At Tichfield the big gate-house became the nucleus of the Southamptons' mansion – one sees three generations of them on their tomb, with obelisks to symbolize eternity. The 'eternity' promised in Shakespeare's Sonnets has proved more enduring – the house is a ruin. In London the refectory within Blackfriars became the private theatre taken over by his company; other houses put up within the precincts belonged to its patron, the Lord Chamberlain, whose mistress the company's playwright took over.

Left Romsey Abbey, Hampshire, a Norman abbey church lying on the edge of the New Forest.

Right Tewkesbury Abbey in Gloucestershire was purchased by the townsfolk after the Dissolution of the Monasteries (1536–39).

The country's parish churches, our leading authority, Sir Alec Clifton-Taylor, assures us, offer 'a wealth of architecture which in the entire world is rivalled only by Italy and France'. Today we are to study and enjoy them, he recommends, as works of art: 'Much of what can be seen came into being as an outcome of the sheer joy of creation, like so much of the best art of every kind the world over.' To this we should add competition and rivalry, always an immense stimulus in every sphere, and the imitation of good models set – as we can read in the building accounts of such churches. Social imitation too, as the sociologist Gabriel Tarde pointed out, is a powerful factor in improving people's standards; naturally where this is missing they sag downwards.

Sir Alec Clifton-Taylor emphasizes again the variety given by regional character, different materials, different styles. The most opulent medieval churches are naturally to be found in what were then the richest agricultural areas, since medieval society spent its surpluses on communal works intended to last – not on the trivia of a consumptive society. Thus the largest churches are apt to be in the country round Hull – Hull and Grimsby each has a vast church – such as Hedon and Howden, and in the alluvial soil around the Wash, such as Boston, Terrington St Clement, and Sleaford with its sophisticated west front. The woollen and clothing areas threw up good churches, often the benefactions of prosperous merchants, like Greenway at Tiverton with its ornate sculpture, or Northleach with a series of clothiers' brasses.

We are told that, in this form of art – at its finest in the fourteenth and fifteenth centuries – this country possesses more brasses than the whole of the rest of Europe put together. What a heritage! And this in spite of the fact that the Reformation and the Puritans destroyed hundreds of them. During the Civil War a Cromwellian officer with his helper locked themselves in Lincoln cathedral and levered up scores. Let me cite only a country church in Norfolk, Felbrigg – beautifully watched over by the late, and last, squire – which has an exquisite brass to Sir Simon Felbrigg and his wife, a 'domicella', or lady-in-waiting, to Richard II's beloved queen, Anne of Bohemia.

Since there were several prosperous clothing areas there are many such churches; Halifax has a notable one – but town churches are apt to have been 'interfered with' by the Victorians. Devon has such specimens as Cullompton or Woolborough, with marvellous woodwork, still coloured, a joy to see; Norfolk and the Cotswolds are two other leading areas, with the wolds of Lincolnshire and north Oxfordshire, where we find a group of spires: 'Bloxham for length, Adderbury for strength, and King's Sutton for beauty'.

We are also assured that 'in no other country in the world is the parish church so frequently the visual centre-piece, the dominant building, of a town or, still more often, a village as in England'. Or again one comes across a lonely church in a deserted spot that gives one a clutch at the heart to see. What will happen to them? Sometimes they have something irreplaceable within, a work of art by a non-recurring man of genius. Stow-Nine-Churches in Northamptonshire has a masterpiece by Nicholas Stone, the sculptor: the church understandably locked – during the war the vicar came upon an American soldier with a crowbar intending to lever up the sleeping figure. I know a church which shall be nameless, with a classic Stone monument, standing alone in the fields by a farmhouse, and reached only by a track. As a laureate of contemporary society writes:

Now that the people are emancipated
The churches have all got to be kept locked ...

Some of them have large collections of monuments, scholarly museums in themselves: like Brington of the Spencers in Northamptonshire where their tombs are gathered together; Bottesford of the Rutland family; Exton of the Harringtons; Fawsley of the Puritan Knightleys; Chenies of the Russells; Tawstock in North Devon, in that lovely landscape of the Taw and Torridge, full of Bourchiers and Wrays. One can read much of English history by

The building of Northleach Church in Gloucestershire was made possible by the generous donations of prosperous clothing merchants.

Above left King's College, Cambridge, one of the finest monuments of English Perpendicular architecture, began by Henry VI and completed by Henry VIII. *Above* One of the stained-glass windows in King's College Chapel.

reading the ledger-stones in church or churchyard – a good habit to develop. Sometimes the churchyards themselves are places of beauty, often affecting: the perfection of Bibury or Painswick, the topiary at Long Melford, the standard roses at Chastleton in that perfect grouping of Jacobean house, tiny church like a domestic chapel for the squire, little Queen Anne circular garden, parlour with tea-things laid out looking down upon it. O the intimate beauty of these English scenes!

There are more particular beauties to observe: ironwork, of which the finest masterpiece is the screen across All Saints, Derby, now the cathedral (Bess of Hardwick lies here); such a door as that at Eaton Bray, or little St Thomas's by the station at Oxford. Sir Alec Clifton-Taylor tells us that the glory of Britain's church interiors is in their woodwork – what a tribute to those vanished generations of carvers – the angel-roofs and font-canopies of East Anglia, the rood-screens of Devon, the bench-ends of Cornwall. Everywhere are bosses, carvings and stained glass expressing their beliefs, of gospel-narratives and saints; or gargoyles and misericords no less expressive of their sense of humour.

Rarely one comes upon something gorgeous and sophisticated, like the baroque church beside the burnt-out palace of Witley Court; or the pretty Gothick interior at Shobdon in Herefordshire (the big house gone), like a setting for an intimate eighteenth-century opera. However, a more characteristic choice, to speak of the tides of time, would be a medieval church with all the fittings of the subsequent centuries. Clifton-Taylor's choice is Navestock in Essex; mine would be West Country, Launcells in Cornwall, untouched since Regency days; Molland in north Devon, tiny but packed with woodwork and monuments; and Torbryan in south Devon, whence came the Catholic Petres, with rood-screens, pulpit, bench-ends all perfect, pews lit by candles - everything!

OXFORD AND CAMBRIDGE have been so much written about, and have made such overwhelming impact upon the nation, that here we can do little more than to point out their contrasts. Cambridge was the eastern university, Oxford the western, in days when distances made such a difference to travel. The significant contrasts begin with the Reformation, which made the fortunes of Cambridge, though in the fifteenth century it was beginning to come up fast – one can see that in the patronage of the Lancastrian royal house. Henry VI gave Cambridge the incomparable glory of King's College Chapel, completed by Henry VIII. His grandmother, the Lady Margaret, founded two colleges, St John's and Christ's, while Henry and his daughter made generous benefactions to Trinity. They did nothing much for Oxford; Henry came near to suppressing Wolsey's foundation of Christ Church, instead of completing it.

In the Middle Ages Oxford was one of the foremost universities of Europe, for a century or so – roughly 1300 to 1400 – producing the leading philosophers in the West, mainly Franciscans. Roger Bacon, Duns Scotus, William of Ockham – we still speak of 'Ockham's razor' in logic – are best known. Then came Wyclif, whose influence created a disturbance for orthodoxy, and led to the popular movement of the Lollards, with their vernacular

Right Francis Bacon (1561–1626), the philosopher, statesman, essayist, and lord chancellor of England under James I, attended Trinity College, Cambridge.

translations of the Bible – combustible material. All this led deviously on to the Reformation – Tyndale's translation of the Bible lies behind subsequent versions; its impact was enormous, and he was an Oxford man.

More important than the philosophers were the practical leaders and administrators in Church and State who ran things. The archbishops and their suffragans were overwhelmingly Oxford men; so were the chancellors, treasurers and secretaries who worked the administration. Even before the university took shape in the early thirteenth century, Oxford was a centre of study, around the priory of St Frideswide (which the Reformation made into a cathedral) and the collegiate chapel in the castle (now the gaol). At the latter Geoffrey of Monmouth wrote his *History of the Kings of Britain* which catapulted the 'matter of Britain' – the Arthurian stories – into all the literatures and arts of Europe.

The Reformation had revolutionary effects upon religion and education. Medieval universities were like modern, with students milling about the streets undisciplined – and for a comic view of what went on read Chaucer's naughty Tales dealing with Oxford and Cambridge. The Elizabethans expanded the colleges to bring students inside, discipline them, teach them more efficiently and train them up to be more useful servants of Church and State. The Elizabethans were strenuous believers in education, especially for the operative classes. Feudal nobles had been mostly illiterate; very exceptional was a knight like Sir Thomas Malory, who could write, and with such a gift of style. Now the sons of nobility and gentry were sent to the university to equip themselves – Essex, Sidney, Southampton, Ralegh, Cecils, Bacons - not only those who were to serve the church or the professions.

Easterly Cambridge was more exposed to Continental winds blowing in, from both Luther and Calvin. Where Oxford favoured Catholic reformers – Colet, founder of St Paul's School, Sir Thomas More and his friend Erasmus, cardinals like Wolsey and Pole – Cambridge took the Protestant lead and produced the Protestant martyrs, Cranmer, Latimer, Ridley, invidiously burnt at Oxford. All the Elizabethan archbishops were Cambridge men; so were the leaders of the state, Cecils, Bacons, Walsingham. Cambridge then became the intellectual focus of Puritanism, with Thomas Cartwright – against the philosophic Richard Hooker who made the classic case for the Anglican *via media* ('middle way'). Cambridge produced Oliver Cromwell and John Milton; Oxford was the Royalist capital during the Civil War.

We observe the different inflexions developing. Since Cambridge had been more Protestant and Puritan, it became more Latitudinarian and Whig; along with this developed the scientific inflexion – Isaac Newton was an easterner, from Lincolnshire. In Newton and Darwin, Cambridge put forward the most influential scientists of all; its record in the physical sciences is incomparable.

Oxford was more conservative, royalist and high church – Laud and Newman are prominent figures here; thus more historically minded, leaning to politics and the humanities. Hobbes and Locke are seminal minds in these fields; Locke was virtually an opposite number to Newton, with enormous influence in both philosophic and political thought – he also wrote on education – throughout the eighteenth century at home and abroad. Blackstone was hardly less of an authority on the law, in both England and America, until Bentham gave the main intellectual impulse to nineteenth-century reform. We see that Oxford's strength was in the humanities – again with the first historian in Gibbon, and the orientalist Sir William Jones, who codified Moslem and Hindu law for India, resuscitated Sanskrit and effectively sowed the seeds of Indian nationalism.

In the realm of religion John Wesley – whose background was high church, even Jacobite, and he remained always an authoritarian Tory – created a world church with Methodism. The Wesleys were very Oxonian, a wonderful family: two of Britain's best hymn-writers, and S. S. Wesley. In the nineteenth century Newman started a whole movement in the Church, its intellectual effects more widespread and significant than Wesley's in the world today.

'Tom Tower' of Christ Church, Oxford, built by Christopher Wren.

Desiderius Erasmus
(*c.* 1466–1536) brought
Humanism to Oxford and
Cambridge through his
lectures there during the
Renaissance. It was at Oxford
that he met Sir Thomas More.

In the twentieth century the situation has become more complex. Cambridge took the lead in philosophy and economics. Conversely, Oxford took the lead in chemistry, where Cambridge held it in physics and mathematics. It was in the Cavendish Laboratory that the atom was split and our brave new world of nuclear fission was inaugurated. Oxford has gone in for bio-chemistry and medicine, discovering penicillin and opening up the universe of anti-biotics to bring relief to millions of suffering humanity throughout the world.

However, we must not forget that Sir William Harvey, discoverer of the circulation of the blood, who came over to Oxford as a Royalist, was a Cambridge man. It took a generation before people saw the point of his discovery.

The ancient universities remained closely tied to the Church: most fellows of colleges had to be in orders and undergraduates had to be Anglicans. The reforming zeal of the early nineteenth century, inspired by Philosophic Radicalism, founded University College, London, to provide for those who did not wish to subscribe to Anglican tests. Thus University College provided a new inflexion, with the scientific work carried forward by such spirits as Francis Galton and Karl Pearson in statistics and eugenics. King's College, London, was the Anglican reply to University College's Gower Street following of Jeremy Bentham. Since then the University of London has proliferated in every direction – particularly science, with the Imperial College of Science and Technology. It has hospitals, colleges for women, schools of art like the famous Slade School, and has become one of the largest universities in the world.

A third university might have developed in London much earlier out of the Elizabethan foundation of Gresham College, which was set up with seven professors to give lectures. Those appointed were the most eminent men in their subjects – such as Dr John Bull, composer of genius and a fabulous executant on organ and virginals. In the seventeenth century Robert Hooke and Christopher Wren were professors. In the unreformed eighteenth century the City authorities allowed this promising institution to lapse.

During the Commonwealth it was proposed to make Durham a third university, for the north, but the project did not come about until the reforming 1830s. It has always had the advantage of that marvellous setting – cathedral, castle, and close – to give it the finest campus in the country. The growing prosperity of the Victorian Age released a demand for university education and institutions in its leading provincial centres: hence the colleges founded in Manchester, Liverpool, Leeds, Sheffield, Birmingham, Newcastle upon Tyne, out of which universities developed.

The movement for these civic universities appealed to local pride and incentive; in turn they generated much idealistic enthusiasm. The late Victorians believed in education, with heart and soul, as the Elizabethans had done. One is impressed by the public spirit that inspired and sustained that generation of founding fathers, a remarkable body of principals and vice-chancellors, mostly from Oxford, with a creative job to do. Manchester acquired a certain primacy and prestige in its heyday; it formed a leading History School, virtually an extension from Oxford, as its physics department was from Cambridge.

THE ROYAL COLLEGE OF PHYSICIANS goes right back to the reforming days of Henry VIII; it was founded by Thomas Linacre, one of the Oxford group inspired by the Renaissance and his years in Padua. During that time he translated the works of Galen from Greek into Latin, and thus made the most important medical and anatomical knowledge of antiquity available to the backward medieval world. Surgeons were for long regarded by physicians as inferior. Letting blood, which was their prime occupation in the primitive state of knowledge, more folklore than anything, equated them with barbers, who often did the job as well – hence the red 'bandages' revolving on a barber's pole. These crafts were organized together in the Company of Barber-Surgeons, whom the Royal College of Physicians harassed all it could, along with 'free-lancers' like Simon Forman. Not until 1800 did the Royal College of Surgeons come into existence, propelled by the eminent John Hunter, who left it his remarkable anatomical collections.

Most famous of these bodies is the Royal Society, which was formed at the Restoration, and with the personal interest of Charles II – more amused by scientific experiment than the theological fancies which had convulsed the realm. Before his return, some elect spirits, sick and tired of useless speculations and disputes, came together to investigate the phenomena of nature as they are, not as people supposed them teleologically to be. A group formed at Oxford around the admirable John Wilkins, with others who found London too disturbed and disturbing. The programme was entirely in accord with the ideas advanced by Francis Bacon – the investigation of nature to *improve* man's lot. The objective was carried forward in the official name of the institution, 'The Royal Society of London for Improving Natural Knowledge'. It became the most famous scientific body in the world, and has suggested other similar foundations, such as that in Berlin which was revived by Frederick the Great after his father's suppression of it.

A smaller scientific body, founded for the promotion and popular diffusion of science, is the Royal Institution, in its distinguished building in Albemarle Street. Its fortune was made by the brilliant lectures of Sir Humphry Davy,

> *Who lived in the odium*
> *Of having discovered sodium.*

He discovered many other things, principally in the newly developing field of electricity; but was surpassed by his assistant and successor, Michael Faraday, less brilliant but who gave his genius wholly to his work, and to whom social life and success meant nothing.

QUITE THE MOST FAMOUS of English schools is Eton, since the early nineteenth century the school *par excellence* of the British aristocracy and governing class. It was not always so: in the later seventeenth and much of the eighteenth centuries, from the time of the celebrated headmaster Richard Busby, Westminster prevailed, with its proximity to the seat of government, the Houses of Parliament, and the abbey for its chapel. Nor is Eton by any means the oldest of English schools: it is in a sense a daughter of Winchester College, which had been founded by the big-minded bishop, William of Wykeham, who set the model with his school as a nursery for his college at Oxford, New College. This is properly called New, because it formed the pattern for the subsequent foundations at both Oxford and Cambridge, when the earlier model had been Merton.

Winchester still retains its medieval nucleus, hall, chapel, chambers – it even has, or had, a vocabulary of its own, 'Notions', interesting linguistically – and much that was rather

The largest public school for boys in England is Eton College, Berkshire. It was founded simultaneously with King's College, Cambridge, by Henry VI.

monastic, or distinctly hardy, in its way of bringing up boys. It is popularly held, quite mistakenly, that the public schools were more luxurious than the state schools. The converse is the truth. The public schools were distinctly tough, conditions as harsh as the boys were hardy, with a strong emphasis on sport. In the rough-and-tumble of such a training the upper classes learned team-work and how to pull together – invaluable to a governing class that was to rule not merely a small country but a large empire.

This is the truth behind the historic cliché that Waterloo was won in the playing fields of Eton – well known to Hitler; Germany would have won her game if she had had such a governing class with such training. Actually Eton was a hardy school, particularly strenuous for the masters, a number of whom were celebrated in their own right, admired by their former pupils making their mark in the world. Eton was, and is, a world in itself – rather like a university – and also distinctly worldly; of course it is a distinct advantage in the higher

strata of English life, literary as well as political, to have been at Eton or Winchester.

Naturally I should much have preferred to be in college with the scholars at Eton or Winchester, which collect the cleverest boys in England – and the places are so incredibly beautiful, bound to leave a mark on any boy of historic sense and sensibility. This is especially the case with Eton for its situation by the Thames, that noble chapel, with the medieval frescoes, signalling across the meadows to Windsor and St George's chapel upon its cliff. The Lancastrian Henry VI founded Eton in 1440 and King's College for his scholars to proceed to at Cambridge. The Yorkist Edward IV rebuilt St George's in rivalry – one sees what beneficent results competition produces for society, what an incentive it constitutes. This has been a strongly operative factor all through the English educational system in its best days – though no one has observed it, or commented on its effects, or drawn the obvious conclusions.

One says 'the educational system', but the immense advantage England has had is in the diversity and variety of English schools, as against Continental uniformity. The public schools are those which have been so much admired abroad. In the United States they have been taken as models for such schools as Groton or St George's; the influence of Dr Arnold of Rugby was enormous. Germany attempted – too late – to imitate with Schloss Salem; its inspirer, Kurt Hahn, chose to leave the country and transpose his blueprint to Scotland with Gordonstoun.

The courtyard of Westminster School, beside Westminster Abbey in London.

The influence of the Renaissance, with its emphasis on humanistic Greek and Latin (as opposed to medieval scholastic Latin), can be seen in John Colet's founding of St Paul's School. Paulines have always produced excellent classical scholars – Milton was one. Westminster School was refounded at Elizabeth's accession, after the extinction of Mary's out-of-date monastery; there had been, however, a medieval monastic school, as in many places. With the foundation or refoundation of Charterhouse, Christ's Hospital, and Merchant Taylors', London achieved its complement of famous schools. These, particularly Merchant Taylors' and St Paul's, made the performances of plays – training their pupils in elocution, deportment and public speaking – a notable feature, and they had a formative part in the development of the Elizabethan drama. The boys' companies were serious competitors of the adult public companies – the contest is reflected upon in *Hamlet*. Again we see the stimulating effects of competition.

The Reformation made for revolutionary changes in society; during the 1540s and 50s there was much disarray, and for a time considerable losses in education, in regard to elementary education particularly, though the universities were also hit temporarily. With the stability and gathering prosperity achieved by Elizabeth I's reign, education advanced by leaps and bounds. The universities recovered, increased their numbers and throbbed with vitality. An immense campaign of founding new grammar-schools, or refounding old ones upon firmer, endowed foundations, forged ahead. The campaign was well begun under Edward VI – hence the considerable number of grammar-schools under his name, like the distinguished one at Birmingham.

By the end of Elizabeth I's reign most of the leading towns in most counties had a grammar-school established in them; and the campaign was pursued well into the seventeenth century, especially in backward areas like Lancashire, right up to the Civil War. Reaction set in with the Restoration. City companies, successful merchants, local gentry, bishops, all took a hand in the good work of renewing society, rendering it more efficient, developing its real resources – that is, abilities where they existed – equipping people for its expansion in every sphere. One can trace the enthusiasm released in many towns, often registered on painted boards of benefactors in the parish churches – as at Basingstoke, for example. Or consider the Elizabethan foundations at Tiverton – not only the most historic school in the West Country, Blundell's, but an elementary school, and two or three sets of almshouses.

A game of hockey in front of Charterhouse School, which began its life after an endowment enabled it to be built in the City of London, near Aldersgate. In 1872 it was removed to Godalming in Surrey.

Some of these grammar-school foundations, intended primarily for their localities, became public schools. The best-known instances are Harrow and Rugby, both founded as grammar-schools in the Elizabethan age. Repton was founded as such in 1556, to make use of the disused priory buildings. This practice put such premises to advantageous use in several places – for instance, Sherborne: the monastic school was re-established by Edward VI and the school took over the monastic buildings. At Abingdon Roysse's Grammar School is just outside the abbey gateway. At Canterbury King's School occupies most of the buildings of the former cathedral monastery, as also at Worcester and other places. It was all very convenient, economically more productive, and progressive. No wonder Elizabethan society was the most efficient existing in Europe at the time, and had such achievements to its credit.

The Victorian Age was another such age of expansion, on an enormous scale: the heyday of Britain, when it was the workshop of the world. This in itself meant a bounding growth in prosperity and in the numbers of the middle and professional classes, though landed aristocracy and gentry, even the Church, joined in the general euphoria. One can *see* this alike in the Victorian restoration and building of churches all over the country, and in the growth and founding of public schools. The low point in education was reached in the early nineteenth century; historic schools were down in numbers to a mere score or two of boys. Never was reform more necessary. But it was on the way. Oxford and Cambridge began to shake themselves out of torpor in the early 1800s. Haileybury College was founded by the East India Company in 1809 to train youths who would serve so notably for generations in India (it is amusing that Attlee, who handed over the British Empire in India to their own more drastic imperialism, was a Haileyburian).

Harrow School was founded by John Lyon (died 1592) to educate the children of Harrow. The main school buildings are nineteenth century but the old Fourth Form Room dates from 1611.

Left The Norman Staircase at King's School, Canterbury, which occupies most of the buildings of the former cathedral monastery.

Expansion, prosperity, self-confidence, reform, these were the key-notes of the Victorian Age. The growth of the middle classes and the demand for education are reflected in the reshaping of old schools or the founding of new. The provost of Oriel, which took the lead at Oxford, said that if Arnold – he was a Wykehamist – was made headmaster of Rugby, he would change the face of the public schools throughout England. In fact many remarkable men joined in: Edward Hawtrey at Eton, Edward Thring at Uppingham, E. W. Benson at Wellington. Cheltenham started in 1841, Marlborough in 1843, Radley in 1847, Lancing in 1848. There followed other schools founded by Nathaniel Woodard, while Uppingham, Oundle, Dulwich, Tonbridge, Sedbergh, and so on, were either new or re-made.

Elementary education lagged behind, largely because of the squabble between the religious sects, and the opposition of the Dissenters to any State support that might advantage the Church schools, which were in a large majority. After decades of dispute a national system of elementary education was established by the Act of 1870, brought in by the admirable Quaker, W. E. Forster. He was married to Dr Arnold's daughter, and had the benefit of Matthew Arnold's advice and experience as a life-long elementary school-inspector. The battle for elementary education won, Matthew Arnold spent the rest of his official life campaigning for a national system of secondary education – the extension of grammar-schools, in the renovated image of the public schools, all over the country. This was accomplished by the Education Act of 1902, under the guidance of a powerful civil servant, with immense drive, Sir Robert Morant (another Wykehamist). The establishment of new schools released a flood of local enthusiasm and idealist public spirit all over the country, especially in backward areas like Cornwall where educational opportunities had remained very restricted. I saw something of the spirit at work in Sir Arthur Quiller-Couch, himself a product of Clifton, started in 1862, under the influence of Arnold's Rugby.

Good standards were what these people stood for and inculcated; they were liberal-minded and progressive at the same time as they appreciated the values of the historic and the traditional. Values are the subtlest of all elements for a society to imbibe and transmit: these are the most precious of all transmitted by our ancient universities and schools, which have shown themselves at all stages willing to take part in the continuous work of handing them on to new – if these are permitted and willing to receive.

6 TECHNOLOGY AND THE ARTS

LITERATURE HAS BEEN THE CHIEF CONTRIBUTION of the English-speaking peoples in the sphere of the arts – and it was so right back with the original Anglo-Saxons, who have left us a more important body of poetry than any other of the early Teutonic peoples. Crossed with Celtic influences, as in the visual arts, this has made for a rich heritage indeed. Among European literatures only French can be compared with it, superior in prose, where English has been remarkable more for its poetry.

Some have wondered why a people who have been considered essentially practical and have thrived (in the past) in trade, shipping and industry should have produced such a poetic heritage. But the two things go, or went, together: they were two aspects of the same concrete and creative imagination. Something profound also is due to the nature of the language: the cross-fertilization of Teutonic with Romance elements produced a not thoroughbred but very flexible, various and expressive language, both practical and quick, but also suggestive and poetic, illimitable in its possibilities. French, more thoroughbred, is more limited, the language for prose; English is the language for business, politics and poetry.

Here we are to consider the matter visually. We cannot do justice to the theme aurally. We can, however, say that there is vastly more variation of speech within this small island than in the whole area of the United States. (American variations of English offer an extension of our theme.) There is not only English but the Celtic languages of the predecessors of the Anglo-Saxons in the island, whom they largely dispossessed: Welsh and the Gaelic of Scotland (the Cornish language is a dialect of the first, Manx of the second). Within English itself there are numerous dialects, with their differing accents and vocabularies: the main division being – as also in history – between south and north, but also a marked division between east and west. How many the variations are may be seen from a small county like Cornwall, where there is a distinct difference between west and east Cornish dialect, the latter approximating to west Devon speech. Such dialectal variations exist within every county. No wonder the *English Dialect Dictionary*, in several large volumes, was a landmark of scholarship!

Previous pages The Clifton Suspension Bridge over the Avon at Bristol, one of the masterpieces of Isambard Brunel (1806–59).

Right William Shakespeare, whom Ben Jonson prophetically described as being 'not of an age, but for all time'.

Left The room in which Shakespeare was born at Stratford-upon-Avon.

Dialect literature has not been of the first importance in Britain, except for Lowland Scots – and the Scots would, rightly, not regard their speech as a dialect. It is the proper descendant of the Anglian speech of the north, and it has a considerable literary heritage, in which Robert Burns and Walter Scott stand out as peaks. Literary Anglo-Saxon is represented by the Wessex dialect of Somerset and Dorset, which produced an admirable poet in the Victorian, William Barnes, mentor of Thomas Hardy. Standard English is the Mercian language of London, and the central importance of London is witnessed by this fact.

We are, then, to think of literature visually in terms of place. Here again London is overwhelming – newcomers naturally found their inspiration there from Scots Dunbar to American T. S. Eliot. This has been continuously so from the time of Chaucer and Langland, both of whose work is full of London. Langland was a chantry-curate in the city; Chaucer, son of a London vintner, lived for years in Aldgate; Gower lived in Southwark and is buried in the cathedral.

Court literature was essentially directed to the London-Westminster axis, as we see with Chaucer, or again with Skelton, an East Anglian whose fortune was made by his Court connection. We see it again with the Elizabethans, with Sidney and Spenser:

Sweet Thames, run softly till I end my song.

Spenser was London bred and educated, at Merchant Taylors' School. Shakespeare was essentially a countryman – one sees that in all his work – with a Warwickshire background; but the London theatre made his fortune for him, and there is no more convincing portrayal of life in Elizabethan London than the roistering of Falstaff and his companions, the scenes at the Boar's Head in East Cheap in *Henry IV*. Ben Jonson, of Scottish Borderer stock, was London born and educated (at Westminster School); his work is similarly inspired, with London types in *Volpone* and *The Alchemist*, and scenes such as *Bartholomew Fair* presents. His masques belong to Court literature.

Samuel Johnson (1709–84), the outstanding man of letters of the eighteenth century, whose life was chronicled by his friend James Boswell.

Restoration literature was more geared to London than even Elizabethan literature had been – not only the drama but the poetry and satire of Dryden. Addison's historic importance – for which he received much credit and a measure of veneration – was to put civilized urban standards via *The Spectator* across to his readers all over the country. Of the novelists, Richardson was a life-long Londoner, a printer; Fielding made his living by the London stage and journalism, and ended as a Westminster magistrate. Pope never moved far from the banks of the Thames, in his life or in his work.

London proliferates in the literature of the nineteenth century: naturally with the novelists, Dickens, Thackeray, Trollope, Henry James, but with the poets too. The ground of attack on Keats was that his was 'Cockney' poetry, like Leigh Hunt's or Thomas Hood's. But a grander spirit like Wordsworth has a London section of *The Prelude*, or a sonnet such as that 'Composed upon Westminster Bridge'.

> *Earth has not anything to show more fair:*

or 'London, 1802':

> *Milton! thou shouldst be living at this hour:*
> *England hath need of thee . . .*

All the Rossettis were Londoners; visitors and temporary residents drew inspiration or paid tribute: Yeats wrote 'The Lake Isle of Innisfree' going up Ludgate Hill, and Bridges produced a wonderful evocation in 'London Snow'.

160

In our time H. G. Wells was a Londoner bred, his London novels his best, a lesser Dickens. Shaw and Bennett, Galsworthy and Somerset Maugham, Belloc and Chesterton all came to London to make their name – needs must for theatre people like Wilde, Pinero, Barrie, Nöel Coward, Ivor Novello and their successors. The same held good for painters and, to a lesser extent, musicians – Elgar wrote his *Cockaigne Overture*, Vaughan Williams his *London Symphony*. A whole literary and artistic faction grouped itself around 'Bloomsbury', in spite of disclaimers.

Second in importance and inspiration comes Edinburgh, naturally enough, for it too was a capital. We have pointed to its most brilliant period, the later eighteenth century, but the glow continued well into the nineteenth – till the death of Scott in 1832 – with the rival Whig periodical, *The Edinburgh Review*. This was the organ of Francis Jeffrey, Sydney Smith and Macaulay, as also of the early Carlyle. He did not really fit in, having an original message all his own. Not far away were the 'Lakers' – in the Lake District where Wordsworth settled, and whence he drew inspiration for much of his work. Here he was joined permanently by Southey, intermittently by Coleridge and his son Hartley, by Hazlitt, De Quincey and others. All of these owed something of their work to that background.

Other areas, other literary provinces. The most authentic and convincing is Hardy's 'Wessex', the novels conveniently provided with a map. Trollope's cathedral city, Barchester, the life within and the country neighbourhood around are very much of the

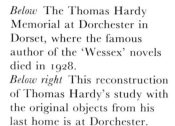

Below The Thomas Hardy Memorial at Dorchester in Dorset, where the famous author of the 'Wessex' novels died in 1928.
Below right This reconstruction of Thomas Hardy's study with the original objects from his last home is at Dorchester.

south-western counties. The background of George Eliot's earlier novels is west Midlands; farther west, Severn country for A. E. Housman and Masefield. The West Riding of Yorkshire is Brontë country; Nottingham and Eastwood, the Notts–Derbyshire border, D. H. Lawrence's; South Wales belongs to Dylan Thomas. These are only a few examples, not exhaustive, of the provincial inheritance – landscape, character, speech – that has gone, along with London and the cities, into our literature.

THE ARCHITECTURAL HERITAGE is so familiar to us as to be almost part of the landscape. No English village is complete without its church, no landscape without tower or spire; the skyline of towns and cities today is in confusion, churches with their belfries put out of countenance by high-rise buildings, out of all proportion – but then all now is out of the human scale.

The Victorians admired the Early English style almost to excess: high vaults, narrow arches, tall lancet windows. Actually Perpendicular was England's speciality in medieval building, secular as well as ecclesiastical: an almost classic form of Gothic achieving a perfect balance between horizontal and vertical. One sees it magnificently in such grand halls as that at Trinity College, at King's College Chapel at Cambridge, in the Divinity School as well as the nave of St Mary's at Oxford; in halls like Westminster or Dartington or Penshurst as well as in the chancel at Gloucester cathedral where the style was formed. The Elizabethans made something quite special out of it. Their architectural achievement has been depreciated as neither purely Gothic nor yet achieving classicism. Though they were very experimental, they knew what they wanted; and in their finest houses, Hardwick, Burghley, Hatfield, Wollaton, Kirby (Theobalds, Holdenby, Wanstead, Basing, even Audley End, have largely gone), they achieved something original, with its own style. It is absurd to question it, for anyone with an eye can recognize an Elizabethan house when he sees one. These palaces express the fantasy, the soaring ambition, the inspiration of the age in their way, as the *Faerie Queene* or *King Lear*, Ralegh's *History of the World* or Bacon's *Novum Organum* do in theirs.

The full classical impact of the Mediterranean world came with Inigo Jones, who spent years in Italy. Already in the next generation, with Wren, it undergoes a modification: the innate Gothic instinct comes welling up in the fantasy of his spires. Open-minded and compromising as he was – very English traits, and no one was more English than Wren (Inigo Jones was Welsh, Vanbrugh Dutch) – Wren was well capable of building in Gothic style when desired: look at Tom Tower at Oxford. In the next generation again, at the height of the Augustan Age, Gibbs – a Scottish Catholic – was equally open-minded. The Radcliffe Camera in Oxford is the most Roman building in Britain, but with St Martin-in-the-Fields he adapted the spire to a classic portico. Described as 'the most important architectural innovation of the century', it was immensely influential throughout the old empire. 'The supreme symbol of Georgian architecture in its imperial phase', it is again an English compromise between unremitting classicism and the native Gothic instinct.

We have noted the landscape garden, regarded as a work of art, as being an English creation. It often appears in eighteenth-century paintings of landscapes as such, as background to family groups out of doors, conversation pieces, or as decoration in individual portraits – particularly with Gainsborough. History painting was regarded as the summit of achievement; religious painting had been inhibited by Protestantism, and fresco had to be revived under foreign influence, to be taken up notably by Sir James Thornhill for Wren's St Paul's and the hall of Greenwich Hospital.

The British concentrated on portrait and landscape painting: this is where the heritage is richest. Scots and Welsh contributed: Allan Ramsay is among the most charming of portraitists, while no one has ever portrayed character more powerfully than Sir Henry

The splendid nave at King's College Chapel in Cambridge exemplifies the Perpendicular style at its latest.

163

The Radcliffe Camera in Oxford, a masterpiece of
the architect James Gibbs (1683–1754).

Raeburn; Richard Wilson, who was Welsh, was virtually the initiator of English landscape painting. In portraiture there was the English fascination for character to go upon – it comes out again in the diversity of the English novel. In the Elizabethan Age portrait painting was all in all – no one has rendered character more sensitively than the miniaturists Nicholas Hilliard and Isaac Oliver, or later Samuel Cooper (see his portrait of Oliver Cromwell).

The tradition gathered impetus all through the eighteenth century to achieve its height of authenticity with Hogarth and, later, Raeburn. The sitters saw themselves somewhat more ideally with Reynolds and Gainsborough, Romney and Lawrence – as Vandyke had romantically idealized the Court of Charles I. In the later eighteenth and earlier nineteenth century, landscape painting came up to surpass portraiture in the noblest pictures of Gainsborough, Constable and Turner. These in turn were a revelation to the Continent like that of Shakespeare, Scott and Byron, and powerfully encouraged the Romantic Movement that dominated the century in various forms. The art of the water-colour was a specifically English one, hardly known in France until Waterloo and the end of the Napoleonic Empire opened the Continent to these influences. One can read how diversely powerful they were in literature, painting and music with Victor Hugo, Delacroix, and Berlioz.

THE VICTORIES of Trafalgar and Waterloo ended the long French domination of Europe and raised Britain to a peak of prestige which lasted – along with the providential security they

165

gave her – throughout the nineteenth century. The governing class was understandably proud of itself for its long, tough resistance, and the country was proud of the heroic figures who incarnated it, Nelson and Wellington. This national pride was ostentatiously expressed in Trafalgar Square with its overwhelming monument to Nelson, in the funeral ceremonies of Wellington (with Tennyson's 'Ode'), monuments to him everywhere, and the dedication of the big new London railway station. This mood of relief, pride and self-confidence was also behind the reconstruction of Windsor Castle, with the Waterloo Chamber and portraits of Allied potentates, and the replanning of west London. It was a happy inspiration.

Parliament was the political instrument of the governing class which had won so notable a victory against continental absolutism and military dictatorship. Thus the British craft of parliamentary government also enjoyed a century of prestige not only abroad but at home. It was regarded as a model to be followed by the emerging middle classes everywhere, whether appropriate to the conditions of their particular countries or not – very often it was not: it was taken as an aim to be pursued, an objective, and this often served usefully as a lightning-conductor, a deflection from social revolution.

The nineteenth-century cult of parliament involved some rewriting of history – in part it was a 'Whig interpretation' that prevailed. We now know that it was not true that Parliament was the backbone of English history, its constitutional spine. That had always been in the executive, in the hands of the monarchy, except for intervals during minorities or incompetent monarchs, like Henry VI. Even when the Hanoverians came in, on parliamentary terms, there remained a balance between monarchy and parliament right up to George III, after whom the balance shifted decisively to Parliament, which provided even the executive, the monarchy remaining ornamental, though useful.

The essence of parliamentary government, and its prime value in our heritage, have come from its utility in providing something like a consensus in government. This function is expressed in the word itself: after all, it means only an assembly for talking. Consultation and the grant of money for carrying out what the country at large had been consulted upon were its prime functions. The consultation, to be effective, needed to be widely representative; so representation of the people at large more and more widely as the century went on – until we arrived at universal suffrage – became the character of parliamentary institutions and the model many countries sought to follow throughout the world.

The monarchy also had its social utility, after it ceased to provide the functioning executive: first, in so far as it helped, and helps, to keep society together, a symbol of togetherness not only at home but among English-speaking peoples overseas – including even the United States apparently today; second, in so far as it sets good standards – when it doesn't the monarch goes. Even the ornamental, the ceremonial side of this institution with its long historic heritage has its value, as the response to it witnesses. We have visual evidences of all that in coronations, State openings of Parliament, royal occasions, marriages, birthdays, the popular appeal of the regalia in the Tower. And, of course, permanent reminders of the historical evolution of these institutions exist in the buildings. Henry VIII moved into Wolsey's Whitehall – so Whitehall, home of the administrative bureaucracy hived off from that. William III favoured Hampton Court and built Kensington Palace, while St James's was retained in London. George III preferred Windsor and bought Buckingham House, rebuilt by Nash and enlarged by Edward VII, to become the monarch's chief residence. Around the royal park of St James's are other such residences: Marlborough House, built originally by Wren for Duchess Sarah; Clarence House; Lancaster House serves the purpose of government entertaining. It is a pity that the Regent's Carlton House has gone, he had such taste: it stood above the Duke of York's Steps, the columns that decorated it may be seen in front of the National Gallery in Trafalgar Square, looking down to the Nelson Monument, Charles I's statue, Inigo Jones's Banqueting House, William Kent's Horse Guards, Sir Charles Barry's Houses of Parliament, and all that history.

Right The Throne in the House of Lords.

Below The statue of 'Justice' on top of the Old Bailey in London.

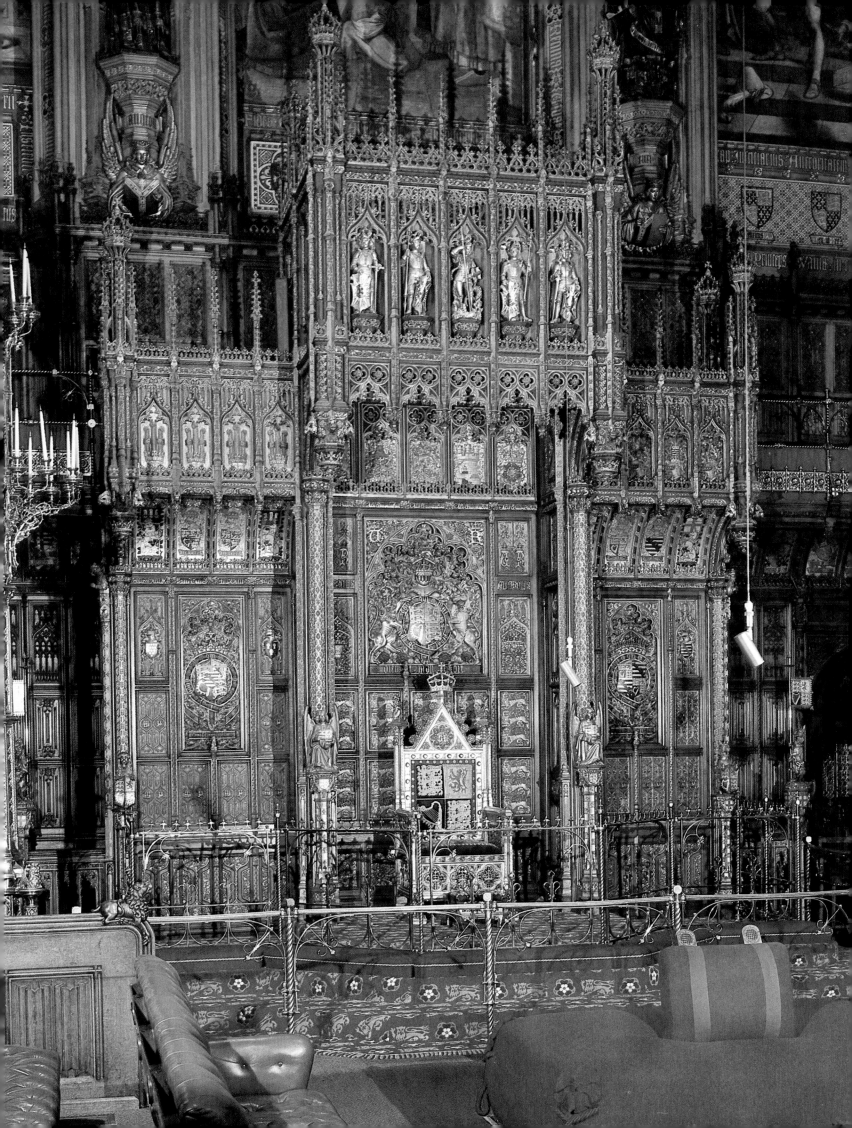

Above British pageantry at its most splendid: the Procession of the Garter, with the Queen at its head, wends its way through Windsor Castle to St George's Chapel.

Right The eastern Lady Chapel, or Henry VII Chapel, in Westminster Abbey, London.

Left 'Bottle ovens' at the Gladstone Pottery Museum, Longton, Stoke-on-Trent. At this working museum one can still see how pottery was produced in the nineteenth century, when the area around Stoke became the centre for the production of pottery. It is still today the home of the greatest names in the manufacture of ceramics of all kinds.

Right The Warehouse at Coalbrookdale in Shropshire, where in 1709 Abraham Darby succeeded in replacing charcoal by coke for smelting in the production of iron. This was to be one of the major contributing factors to the subsequent industrial boom in Britain.

NO LESS IMPORTANT than the political heritage, perhaps even more so, is the industrial: after all, the Industrial Revolution underlies modern industrial civilization, and it was worked out in this small island. Its monuments lie chiefly in the north, in Lancashire and Yorkshire, the northern Midlands, South Wales, the Tyneside and Clyde areas. But indeed, its evidences and relics are everywhere: factory buildings and warehouses – the earlier ones often good pieces of Georgian architecture, like the Methodist chapels that went with them; canals and mill-houses, witnessing the earlier dependence upon water-power; the ruined engine-houses of the mines, such as the romantic shells that decorate the sky-line in Cornwall; the docks and quays of London, Bristol, Glasgow – the progressive deepening of the Clyde to make that a great port is in itself a visual tribute to Scots energy; the cranes and gantries of South Wales, the sad slag-heaps of the Rhondda, the quarries of North Wales, the bridges over the Menai Straits, Severn, Tyne, Forth and Tay as the railways pulled the island together. For, after the canals, and the Duke of Bridgewater, came the railways with Trevithick and Stephenson; the railways remain and the stations, big and small, to remind us of the Railway Age, a high point in Britain's history.

Above A typical landscape at the upper end of the Rhondda valley in Glamorgan, Wales, where villages were built up around the coal mines.

Left Ironbridge in Shropshire was the world's first entirely iron-built bridge, and took only three months to construct in 1780. It was designed by Abraham Darby, founder of Coalbrookdale, and is still in use today.

The quickest way to get a visual impression of all this humming development is to pay a visit to the Science Museums in South Kensington. In themselves we owe them to that age, offshoots of the Great Exhibition of 1851 which advertised the new industrial Britain to the world, while that was owed to the imagination of the Prince Consort. The Science Museums hived off from the original British Museum, when its marvellous collections became too much for it to hold. Similar specialization became necessary with other large collections – for example, at Edinburgh and Glasgow, Oxford and Cambridge, and provincial capitals. London, Edinburgh and Cardiff have national galleries for their pictures, though London has many further offshoots, such as the Victoria and Albert Museum, the National Portrait Gallery, the Tate Gallery, besides subsidiary galleries in Dulwich, Whitechapel and Kenwood House at Hampstead. Similarly in the provinces the growth of collections has necessitated further specialization and the founding of fellow institutions, museums often with a valuable local character and accent (cf. Norwich, Nottingham or Leicester; Bristol, Dorchester, Truro).

Right Flying shuttles from the eighteenth century, in the Science Museum.
Bottom right The Joseph Harrison loom, dated 1851.

One can *see* the evolution in a small area at Oxford: the original collections of the Tradescants, the Pembroke and other marbles, the pictures, in the Ashmolean. The Old Ashmolean has become a museum of old scientific instruments, like the Wellcome Medical Museum in London. Answering the impulse of the early Victorian Age the museum itself was founded under the lead of the redoubtable doctor, Sir Henry Acland, and Ruskin (hence the Venetian Gothic and the sculptural decoration). The concept behind the Oxford Museum, like that of the British Museum – the largest and richest in the world, proliferating from 1753 – was a general one, to include everything of scientific interest, in the widest sense of the word. But at Oxford, as in London and elsewhere, the general museum has had to become the parent of specialized institutions and departments, geological, medical, archaeological, and so on. One can follow the evolution equally conveniently at Cambridge.

To go back to South Kensington – the Geological Museum sprang out of the Geological Survey of Great Britain, the oldest in the world, founded in 1835. Again this is a significant date: it pre-dates by a quarter of a century Darwin's *Origin of Species* (1859) and the full flowering of evolution, with all that flowed from that in shaping the modern mind. The Science Museum adjoining exposes the whole technological equipment of the modern age since the Industrial Revolution. We begin with Newcomen's atmospheric pumping engine of 1735, with the further developments made by Watt, Trevithick and others; these made the Cornish steam-pumping engine the finest in the world. Indeed, it went over the world, was exported to the USA, Mexico, Peru and as far afield as New Zealand – the biggest specimen, which pumped out the whole Haarlem Meer is preserved as a national monument there in Holland.

At South Kensington are exhibited the textile inventions which made the fortunes of Lancashire, Yorkshire, Nottinghamshire: Arkwright's spinning-wheel, Hargreaves' spinning jenny, Crompton's mule. Actually, an Elizabethan clergyman made a stocking-knitting frame long before them, but it was not proceeded with – it was feared that it would put spinners out of work. Just as, again, blood-transfusion was first performed at Oxford in 1665, but was not followed up on account of unaccountable theological prejudice. From textiles to railways: the earliest locomotives in the world are exhibited – one can still see here Stephenson's Locomotive No. 1, which made the success of the Stockton–Darlington Railway.

'The Opening of the First Public Railway, The Stockton and Darlington' a painting by John Dobbin. George Stephenson was the builder of this railway in 1825, and he later also built the Liverpool–Manchester railway.

The Forth Rail Bridge, over the Firth of Forth in Scotland, was one of the first cantilever bridges, and was built in the late 1880s by Benjamin Baker.

Darlington itself is a creation of the Industrial Revolution – it has a superb Early English parish church, with a complete collection of Victorian glass, but overlaid by the cooling towers of a power-station that are a later development of industrialism. Not far away is Middlesbrough, which was a unique example of a Victorian planned town, on a grid iron pattern, with upstanding town hall – appreciatively drawn and described by John Piper. These pieces of Victoriana, railway and all, we owe to the initiative of the remarkable Quaker family of Pease.

Naturally the maritime section at South Kensington is of prime interest for a nation that has lived by its shipping. The historical aspect may best be studied at the fascinating National Maritime Museum at Greenwich, part of that splendid naval complex with its treasures and relics. At the Science Museum we can view the technical side to the story: the

175

Left The telescope put together by Isaac Newton, now in the Science Museum.

Right The Victorian Gothic building of the Natural History Museum, South Kensington, London.

first steamships to make the crossing of the Atlantic, the first screw-steamer to do so, the first sea-going ironclad; models of the Elizabethan sailing ships that sailed round the world and fought the Spanish Armada. There are the later developments of steam-power, the first vessel to be driven by the turbine invented by Sir Charles Parsons, inventor also of the dynamo. In 1914 Great Britain built fifty-two per cent of all the merchant shipping built in the world.

Other sections illustrate more of Britain's astonishing creativeness in the scientific field in the modern era that begins with Galileo, Bacon and the founding of the Royal Society. We can see telescopes made by Newton, optical instruments made by his rival Robert Hooke, astronomical devices of prolific Edmund Halley of Halley's Comet. The little observatory from which he did such valuable work may still be seen on the top of a seventeenth-century house in New College Lane at Oxford. Cambridge is represented by the apparatus used by J. J. Thomson in the discovery of the electron, and part of that which 'split the atom'. We are in the modern nuclear world.

Of the men of genius who have made the scientific heritage of Britain probably the first in the world, we should single out Francis Bacon for his prophetic forecast of what science could do for the amelioration of the human lot (hearing aids, television, refrigeration); and for his ardent programme for the investigation of nature and finding out what things are and how they operate rather than pursuing teleological will-o'-the-wisps, as humanity has done most of the time. Second, we should cite Sir William Harvey, discoverer of the

circulation of the blood – though no one would believe him at the time. Third, Newton not only made fundamental discoveries in mathematics – the binomial theorem, the differential and the integral calculus – and in optics, with regard to the nature of light and colours, but also established the general principle of gravitation which made a Newtonian epoch in scientific thought. Charles Darwin is a fourth figure whose work was similarly epoch-making. Along with his specialist work in geology, zoology and botany, arising out of his researches and discoveries, and confirmed by these, he formed his general theory of evolution by natural selection. The application of this to the descent of man had revolutionary consequences for religion, and for theology in particular; it may be said to have constituted the main intellectual theme of the nineteenth century, as Newtonianism had of the century before.

We may then sum up the main constituents of Britain's heritage, as it has affected the world, as the following. The English language, and that the dominant one of three within the area of a small island, has had the extraordinary fate – owed to its historic expansion – of becoming a world language; its literature a world literature with increasing contributions from the English-speaking world, particularly the United States where the largest number of those who speak the language live. The practical, concrete, realist side of a mixture of peoples whose philosophic expression has been, significantly, empirical and pragmatic, is to be seen in their wonderful inventiveness and proliferating discoveries in science and technology, with radar and penicillin, opening up the universe of antibiotics. Lastly there has been the successful model of government by consultation and consensus, the representative parliamentary institutions which have been taken by so many peoples for model in the outer world. The essence of these, however, is not numbers, the mere counting of heads, least of all in the widening areas of mass-civilization, but responsibility. Responsible, representative government means a two-way responsibility: that of the government to the people at large, and that of the people to the government they have chosen, and which they are free to change.

These things are what chiefly have emerged from Britain's long history: a creditable record for a small island, and a rich heritage to pass on to others.

Previous page A new home for the National Theatre: the recently-completed building is on the south bank of the Thames by Waterloo Bridge, and forms part of the expanding South Bank Arts complex.

ACKNOWLEDGMENTS

Photographs were supplied or are reproduced by kind permission of the following:

Ashmolean Museum,	28
Peter Baker Photography	50, 51, 59, 78, 80 (*right*), 81, 84–5, 89, 95, 98, 101, 104–5, 107, 114–15, 156, 172 (*top*), 175
John Bethell	17 (*bottom*), 97
British Museum	23, 32–3
British Tourist Authority	1, 14, 15, 22–3, 38, 39 (By Courtesy of the Masters of the Bench of the Middle Temple), 41, 45, 46, 52, 53 (*top and bottom*), 56 and 57 (The Dean and Chapter of Durham Cathedral), 60, 61, 70–1, 72, 77, 79 (*top and bottom*), 86, 87, 100, 112, 112–13, 116, 117, 122–3, 127, 133, 135 (The Dean and Chapter of Ely Cathedral), 136, 136–7, 141, 152, 154–5, 160–1, 161 (The Trustees of the Thomas Hardy Memorial Collection, Dorset County Museum, Dorchester), 168, 169, 174
Peter Coats	128
C. H. M. Dobell	151
Robert Estall	10, 11, 12, 16, 18, 82–3, 166, 171, 172 (*bottom*)
Michael Holford	19 (*top*), 21 (*top and bottom*), 26 (*top and bottom*), 27, 29, 30–1 (*top*), 31 (*bottom*), 42–3, 173 (*top and bottom*), 176
Angelo Hornak	8–9, 13, 62–3, 75, 109, 138, 167, 177
A. F. Kersting	17 (*top*), 19 (*bottom*), 20, 24, 33, 40, 66–7, 74–5, 90, 90–1, 93, 99, 102–3, 115, 124, 132 (*left and right*), 137, 148–9, 150, 162, 170, 178–9
Kunstmuseum, Basel	146 (Colorphoto Hinz, Basel)
Jorge Lewinski	6–7
National Portrait Gallery, London	143, 157, 158 (*left and right*), 159, 160
National Trust	43 (*bottom*), 82, 106, 119, 120–1, 121, 123, 125, 129
Photo Precision Ltd	2–3, 34–5, 36–7, 46–7, 48–9, 54–5, 58–9, 64–5, 68, 69, 73, 80 (*left*), 84, 88, 94, 108, 110–11, 118–19, 130–1, 134–5, 139, 142 (*left*), 145, 148 (*bottom*), 153, 164, endpapers
Walker Art Gallery, Liverpool	165
Weidenfeld and Nicolson Archives	142 (*right*)

Picture Research by Linda Proud

INDEX